The Palmistry of Fingerprints

The secret patterns hidden in your fingers and palms

What People Are Saying About

The Palmistry of Fingerprints

As a professional hand reader of over 30 years, this book is easily the best and most ground-breaking work I've ever read. I refer to it constantly as the "bible" of print pattern analysis.
Johnny Fincham (BA), best-selling author of *The Spellbinding Power of Palmistry* and *Palmistry from Apprentice to Pro in Twenty-Four Hours*

Christopher's work on the skin ridges of the palm is a timely and valuable contribution. So much has appeared in journals and on websites and Mr Jones has gathered it all up in a fascinating and comprehensive way. His scholarship of this field is almost overwhelming, but always readable.
Andrew Fitzherbert (BA), professional palmist and author *Hand Psychology* and *The Palmist's Companion*

This is a comprehensive and authoritative book on fingerprint patterns by the world's leading authority on palm reading. It's essential reading for beginners and experienced palmists alike. Until now, this information that fills a long-needed gap in palmistry has been available only to his students. If you're remotely interested in palmistry, you must read this book.
Richard Webster, palmist, mentalist and author of *The Complete Book of Palmistry*

This comprehensive book is an invaluable resource for anyone interested in studying the fingerprints of the hand. I know of no other book which brings together such a well-researched history of fingerprint classifications, statistics of dermatoglyphic distribution, tried and tested in-depth chirological

interpretations of both fingerprints and palmar patterns, with some rare examples, illustrated with ink prints of each feature. Being privileged to own a copy of the original publication I have found it to be THE most useful and interesting book on the subject, suitable for beginners and experts in the fields of handreading, fingerprints and palmar dermatoglyphics.
Lynn Seal, professional handreader since 1988

I am lucky enough to have a first edition of this book. It has been an essential reference for over 30 years and I cannot imagine life without it. Blending elemental symbology, scientific discoveries and a lifetime of research, this new edition will catapult hand readers to the next level of expertise. It's a mind expanding must-read for anyone in our field.
Felicity Booth (MA), professional handreader since 1990, Founding Member of the International Hand Reading Association

The Palmistry of Fingerprints

The secret patterns hidden in your fingers and palms

Your personality and unique identity revealed by the fingerprint and palmar patterns of the hand

Christopher Jones MA (Oxon)

BOOKS

London, UK

Washington, DC, USA

CollectiveInk

First published by O-Books, 2026
O-Books is an imprint of Collective Ink Ltd.,
Unit 11, Shepperton House, 89 Shepperton Road, London, N1 3DF
office@collectiveinkbooks.com
www.collectiveinkbooks.com
www.o-books.com

For distributor details and how to order, please visit the 'Ordering' section on our website.

ISBN: 978 1 80341 996 1
978 1 78099 501 4 (ebook)
Library of Congress Control Number: 2024925556

A CIP catalogue record for this book is available from the British Library.

Design: Lapiz Digital Services

UK: Printed and bound by CPI Group (UK) Ltd, Croydon, CR0 4YY
Printed in North America by CPI GPS partners

Table of Contents

For my old friend Johan Hjelmborg (1948–2023)
Astrologer and handreader extraordinaire

Fingerprints are the residual impression of consciousness seeking expression through your unique incarnation.

Foreword

I began this work in 1991 as a core component for my Advanced Diploma for the Cheirological Society, which required undertaking an original piece of research. At that time, there was very little said about the fingerprints and palmar dermatoglyphics in the teachings of the Society, as emphasis was on the five elements and, particularly, the highly dubious technique of dividing the palm into elemental quadrants. It was not even taught how many different types of fingerprints there are, let alone their distributions. It seemed a perfect area of chirology into which to conduct some research. Having recently completed my degree at Oxford University, I still had access to all the university libraries. As these are copyright libraries, everyone in the UK who publishes a book, scientific paper, newspaper or pamphlet is legally bound to deposit a copy in that library. What that also meant was that every book on handreading, chirology and palmistry that had ever been published in the UK had been deposited there. This is what enabled me to do the research needed for my compendium on *The History of Handreading* (1994), which I wrote during this same period. In addition to all the historical material, the science libraries of the university also carried copies of every scientific, medical, psychology, criminological and anthropological journal that had ever been published in the UK. Amongst these journals lay the many thousands of papers researching the significance of fingerprints and dermatoglyphics which formed the basis of my other self-published tome, *The Science of the Hand* (1993).

The first edition of this book, *The Interpretation of Dermatoglyphic Patterns*, was also published in 1993 and became an essential primer in the Cheirological Society. It transformed how we understood the hand and it completely changed the way we all read hands. What was significant was the reframing of the hand through the dermatoglyphic lens which had, up to that point, been almost completely absent. That, as I have argued ever since, is a very serious omission in *any* system of handreading. In addition, because I had access to the resources of the Bodleian Library, I was able to collate and incorporate into our working chirological knowledge, the findings of anthropologists, forensic scientists and medical dermatoglyphicists, the most interesting and relevant discoveries of theirs being succinctly summarised here. This book was, also, the first ever attempt in any work on handreading to comprehensively outline the psychological meaning and significance of each of the fingerprints patterns as found on each of the fingers.

I am pleased to say that many of my students took this initial work and subsequently made further discoveries about the significance of fingerprints, not least Caroline Abrams in her detailed exposition on the significance of the radial loop fingerprint pattern, published in two Cheirological Society journals in 1998. Whilst I was the first person that I am aware of to develop clarity around the psychological significance of the Radial Loop pattern in around 1985, it was Caroline who developed our understanding of it and we are all deeply indebted to her for her insight.

It has been a great pleasure to revisit this work and amend, update and improve it. Whilst I have ruthlessly deleted the more speculative suggestions from the original, and added more recently made discoveries which I have established as being accurate and useful, I am nonetheless impressed with how much of the original text has withstood the passage of time. I trust that you also will find it adds something worthwhile to your own study of the human hand.

Christopher Jones
Waikino, July 2024

Acknowledgements

There is always the opportunity to omit an important influence when it comes to an author's acknowledgements, particularly since it has now been over 32 years since the first edition of this work was published. Knowing that it is likely I have forgotten many others, I would, however, like to especially acknowledge other members of the UK Cheirological Society from that time such as Johnny Fincham, Felicity Booth, Lynn Seal and Laura Thornton, as well as my mother for her unwavering support of my chirological work over many decades.

This updated and revised edition of *The Interpretation of Dermatoglyphic Patterns* could not have come about without the support of my beloved Morgan, who has provided essential proof-reading and editorial assistance. And my thanks are also due to Kim McGaw and Karen Park whose excitement for chirology inspires me and whose enthusiasm deserves reward. Thank you!

This Is Not Fortune Telling!

The patterns of the hands have always fascinated the human mind. There are references to the lines of the palm in the Bible and in the Rig Veda of India but whilst there are many spurious claims made about the antiquity of the study of palmistry, we know for sure that it has a written history within Europe that goes back to at least the twelfth century. What we see when we look at the writings of the early European palmists is that there is primarily a preoccupation with the line formations in the hand. Because it was thought that the lines are manifestations of the mark that God has made in the palm, so the lines reveal a person's fate and destiny.

"He sealeth up the hand of every man so that all men might know His work" Job 37:7.

Palmistry at this time was called chiromancy, "divination from the hand", and concentrated mainly on predicting how long someone was going to live and the nature and manner of their death. The emphasis was firmly on looking for those specific marks and signs formed by the lines of the hand that predicted marriage and the numbers and types of children for women, and wealth, fortune, promotion and education for men. Due to the dominance of the Roman Catholic church, there was equally a fascination with honour and promotions of an ecclesiastical or religious nature, looking for the sign of the "Great Triangle" in the palm as an indication that you had been blessed by God or a mark of promotion that shows you would become a bishop. Many of the earliest manuscripts were written in monasteries and penned by monks so it is clear that the church authorities were not historically opposed to chiromancy as many have supposed.

Much of the present misunderstanding of the significance of the lines comes from this mediaeval view of the hand and when we study these old texts we find that what they really reveal are the interests of the mediaeval mind and the pre-occupations of feudal life. In a Hobbesian world where life expectancy was around 30 years, the prevalence of disease and the predilection of kings to go to war meant there was a keen interest in knowing whether one would die by the sword or die from falling off a horse or have one's eyes poked out. And in a world where your only economic and social function was reproduction, for a woman to know the number of babies she was going to have was a vital piece of information to provide with your dowry. Such a preoccupation with fatalism reflects the rigidity of the feudal class system of the age, in which little or no social mobility was possible. Life at this time was indeed nasty, brutish and short and ran to a predetermined pattern so it is no surprise that the chiromancy of the day was equally fatalistic and deterministic. The whole approach reflects the fatalism of the age.

This emphasis on the predictive assessment of the lines of the hands continues right through to the seventeenth century, with some interest in the "mounds" or raised areas of the palm and how these related to astrological portents and indications. But as the seventeenth century came to a close and astrology gave way to astronomy, palmistry died a complete death within Europe and almost nothing was written on it for a further two hundred years.

When the subject was revived in the mid nineteenth century, it began as a study of the form and shape of the hand. As scientists were looking to physiognomy to understand human nature, palmists were looking at chirognomy – the shape of the hand, the form of the fingers and fingertips, the nails and the knuckles – and a whole new school of handreading was established by D'Arpentigny and his followers. In addition to that, the predictive aspects of looking at the lines of the hands were also revived and so by the end of the century, there was an explosion of interest in the twin approaches of chirognomy and chiromancy, the modern palmistry that most people are familiar with today.

Widely-believed Myth	But in actual fact....
The lines of the hand tell you how long you are going to live	No. The length of the palmar lines do not indicate the length of your life
The markings in the hand show how you are going to die	No they do not
Your 'fate' can be seen in your hand	Your genetics can be seen in your hand, for health and disease. But not your 'fate'
You can predict the future from the lines of the hands	No, this is not possible. The lines of the hands change over time - and you cannot predict in advance how they might change !
Can you tell if I am going to get married from the hand ?	A better question would be to ask: do you want to get married ?
Can you tell how many babies I am going to have?	As a modern woman, you have contraception available. It's your choice.
Can you tell if I am going to win a fortune ?	No
The lines are formed by folding, by the folding action of the hand	Funnily enough, the lines form on the palms of the hands before the muscles of the hands. So, the lines are present *before* the hand is even capable of movement
Handreading was invented by the gypsies	Palmistry is very old, with a written history going back to at least C12th in Europe
Handreading was banned by the Church	In Europe, the earliest extant texts were written by monks and found in monasteries !
The left hand is what you are born with, the right hand is what you have made of it	You are born with both hands! And both hands are important for interpretation
If you have a simian line, it means you are a monkey	2% of people have Simian Lines. But it's seen in 55% of those with Down's Syndrome

The facts about the myths

But what is interesting to note is that by putting such an emphasis on the shape of the hands and the lineation of the palms, even the most assiduous of the Victorian palmists failed to observe the tiny skin ridge patterns that make up the loops and whorls of the fingerprint patterns. Two of the most famous palmists of the day, Cheiro and William Benham, both include prints of hands within their books in which one can clearly see the fingerprints, yet despite their thorough inspection of hands, they fail to assess, comment on or even notice the fingerprint patterns. Benham's main text was published in 1900 at the very same time that scientific interest in the study of the hand was gathering force – the first book on fingerprints was published in 1892. By the end of the nineteenth century the medical and genetic significance of the skin ridge patterns had been determined and the uniqueness and immutability of the fingerprint patterns were being used by police forces around the world. Even Sir Arthur Conan Doyle and Mark Twain had written stories that featured the use of this new science of fingerprinting. And yet the significance of fingerprints completely escaped the attention of the palmists.

Lines or Fingerprints?

One of the major limitations of palmistry then is that it places an emphasis upon the lines of the hand and, by virtue of this comes the generally held understanding that the lines are indicators of our fate or "destiny". This is what most people think of when they come for a handreading, they want to know what's going to happen to them, what is in store for them.

But what most people are not aware of is that *the lines of the hands change over time.*

This is a very important and significant fact – for if it is true that the lines can change, then it can't be true that the lines reveal a fixed fate or destiny. A fixed, unalterable "destiny" could not be so easily affected by hormonal changes or levels of stress.

Moreover, if it is true that the lines of the hands change over time, then we can't actually make a prediction from the lines

Let's look at some examples:

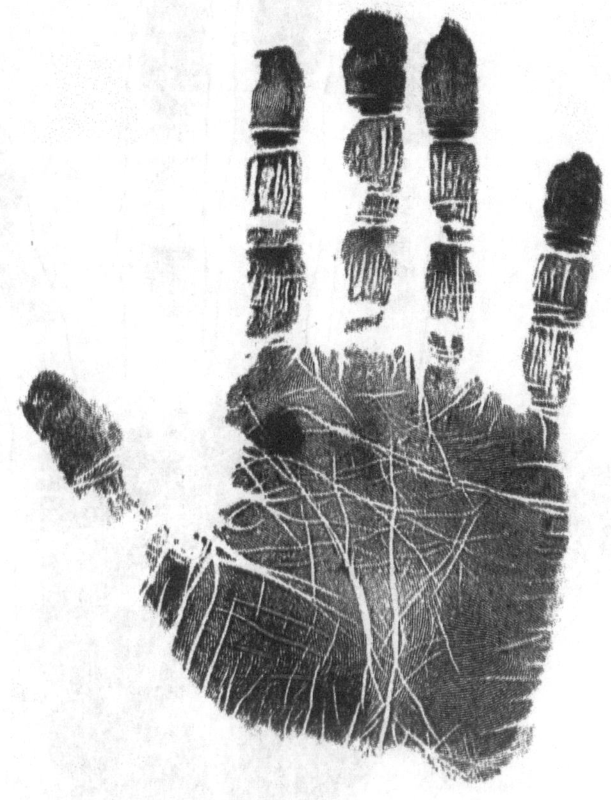

of the hands either. For if the lines change, *we could not possibly know how the lines of the hands are going to change in advance of them changing!*

These handprints are of the same man, with the prints taken in 1972 (aged 26) and 1985 (aged 39). In addition to the many minor line changes, there are also changes to several of the main lines of the hands as well – some have got longer, some have got shorter, some new lines have appeared and some lines have disappeared. We can see that anything we might want to "predict" from the lines of the hand in 1972 might be referencing a line that is no longer present in the hand by 1985! The changes in the lines of the hands that we can see in the above prints is not, of course,

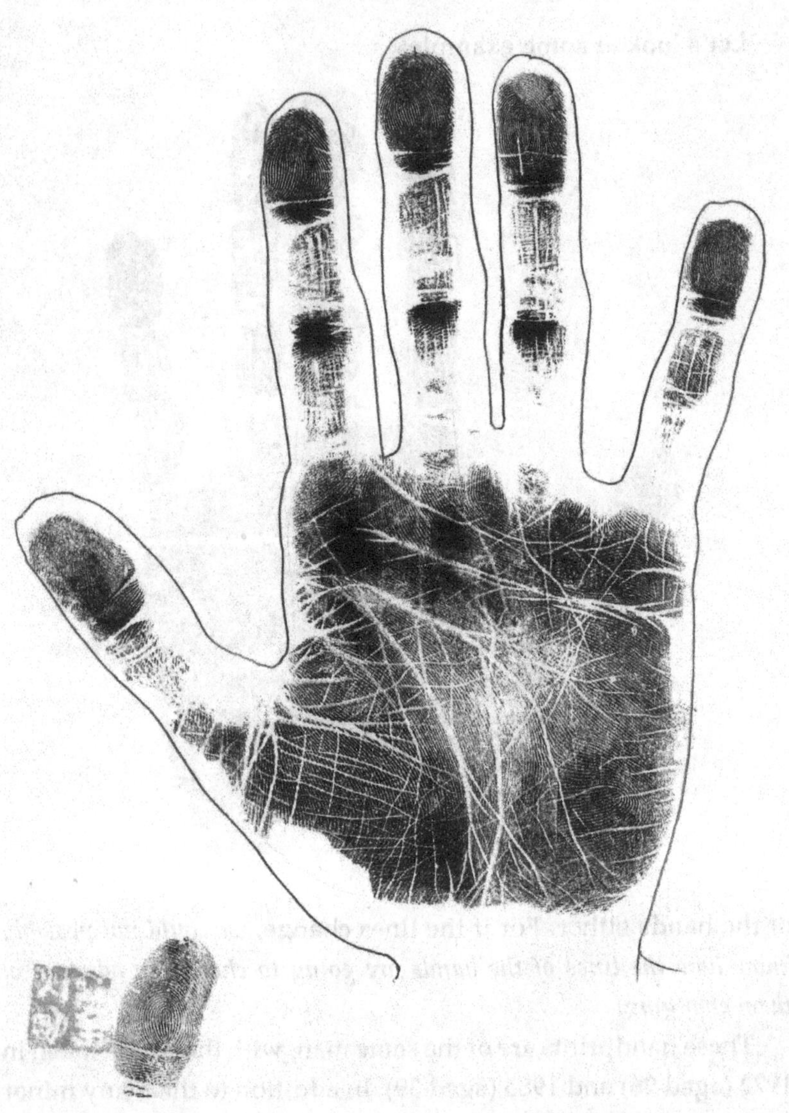

down to changes in the way he has used his hands for the lines in the palm are quite definitely not formed by the folding action of the hands.[1]

In this second example, we have handprints that were taken in 1950, when this man was 29 years old and taken again in 1991 when he was 70 years old. It is obvious, even to the untrained eye, that there

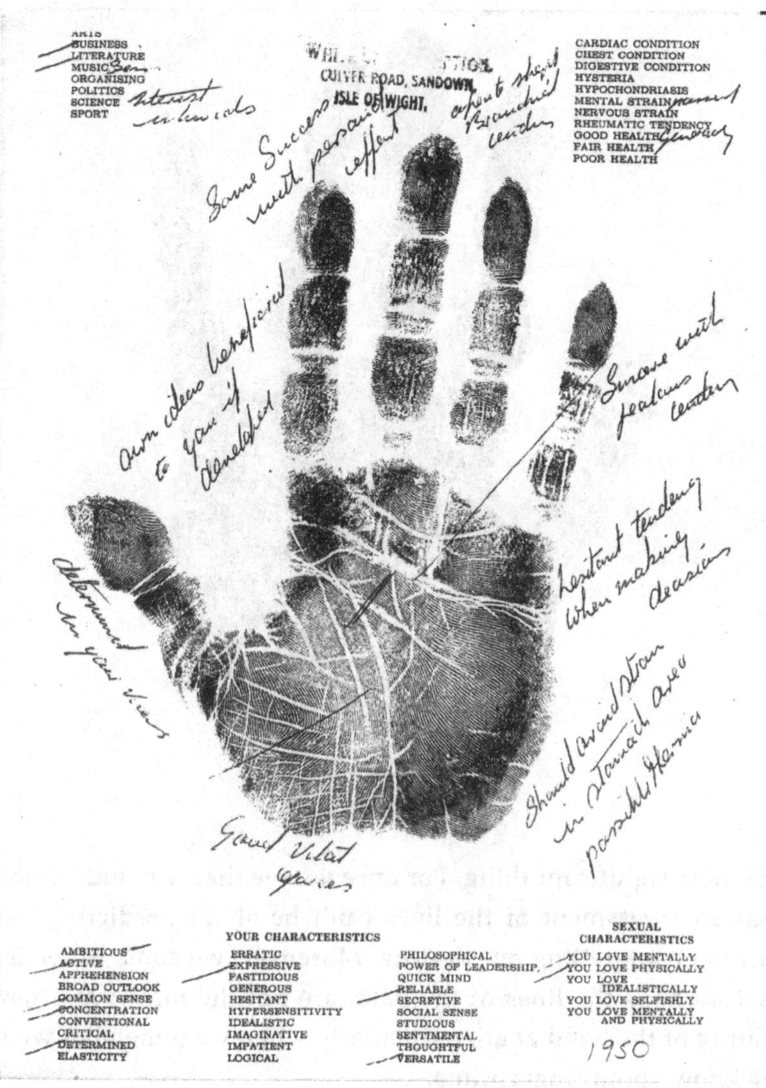

are many changes in the lines of the hands, so many changes in the lines that it becomes clear that the lines of the hand can't *possibly* show the future. There is no way you could "predict" the exact location of where those lines were going to appear 41 years ahead of time.

In fact, it does not matter how much the lines of the hands have or have not changed, the fact that they change at all is

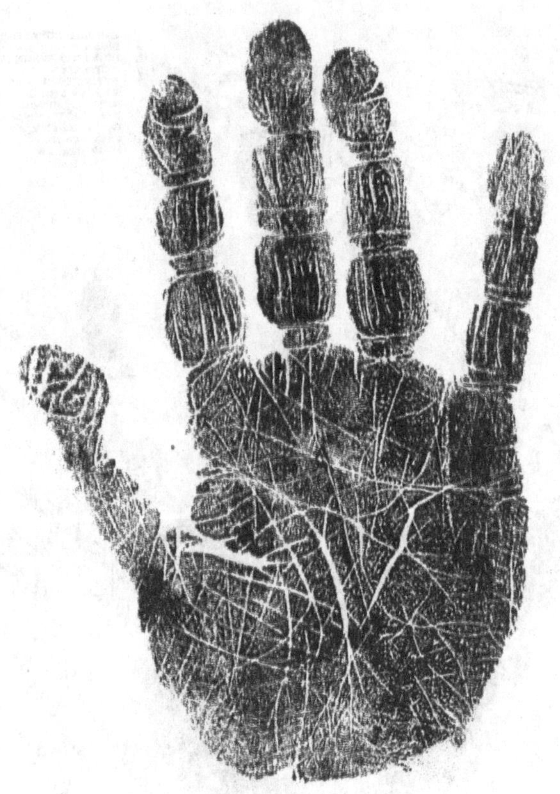

the most significant thing. For once we see that, we understand that an assessment of the lines can't be about predicting our future or foretelling our destiny. Moreover, we come to realise that perhaps the lines of the palm are not the most important feature of the hand at all, particularly when we remember what we know about fingerprints.

For there are two things that everyone knows about fingerprints, the first being that *no two fingerprints are the same.* Everybody has a unique set of fingerprints, so much so that not even identical twins have identical fingerprint patterns.

What everyone is also aware of is that *fingerprint patterns don't change over time.* Many people don't know that they know this – but if you think about it, if that were not true it would be impossible for the police forces and security agencies around the world to use fingerprints for forensic and identification purposes. The unchanging nature of fingerprint patterns shows how much of an important indicator of our identity they are.

That being the case, could it be possible that your fingerprints actually reveal something of your unique identity and what it is to be you?

Let's find out.

1. See Appendix Two *On the Embryogenesis of Lines and Fingerprints*

The Discovery of Dermatoglyphics

Awareness of and interest in the study of fingerprint patterns is a recent phenomenon. Anatomical observations of the skin ridges of the palm were first made as early as the 1680s in works by Nehemiah Grew, Govert Bidloo and Marcello Malphigi, but these amounted to no more than acknowledgements of the existence of these palmar patterns, with a few observations on their uniqueness and variability. **Grew** (1641–1712) was an English doctor and anatomical researcher who presented a report to the Royal Society in 1684 describing the pores of the skin and the skin ridge patterns of the fingers. In 1685, **Bidloo** produced a book on anatomy which included a detailed drawing of a thumb and its dermatoglyphic pattern. In 1686, the Italian anatomist **Malphigi** (1628–1694) commented on the skin ridges of the fingers and their variability in pattern.

Jan Purkinje (1787–1869)

However, no systematic study of the significance of the skin ridge patterns was made until the early nineteenth century. The key figure in the early study of dermatoglyphics was the Czech doctor and researcher **Jan Purkinje**. Purkinje (1787–1869) was working on a thesis about the relationship between the human hand and the eye which was published in 1823 after he had become professor of medicine at Breslau University. The thesis commented on the diversity of the fingerprint patterns and proposed a classification of these patterns into nine types. As we would refer to them now, these were the arch, the tented arch, the ulnar loop, the radial loop, the compound print, the spiral whorl, the elliptical whorl, the circular whorl, and the double loop or composite. Whilst this classification is perhaps a little too elaborate for practical purposes, especially the subdivision of whorls into three types, it is nonetheless more thorough than the later system devised by Galton that has become more widely adopted. Purkinje was also the first researcher to suggest that skin ridge patterns might have both genetic and diagnostic importance.

Towards the end of the nineteenth century, the recognition of the importance of fingerprint patterns was gaining ground in many quarters. The Commissioner for India, **Sir William Herschel**, noticed the use of fingerprints as a form of signature amongst illiterate Indians and successfully employed the use of fingerprints as a means of authenticating the identity of those who worked for him over a twenty-year period. In this time, he also established that they didn't change their form over time, and thus could be relied on as a means of identification. In Japan, a Scottish medical missionary by the name of **Henry Faulds** noticed the use of fingerprints as a form of signature on pieces of pottery and ceramics, and in 1880 he wrote a piece for *Nature Magazine* suggesting that as fingerprints were quite individual, they might successfully be employed in criminal identification.

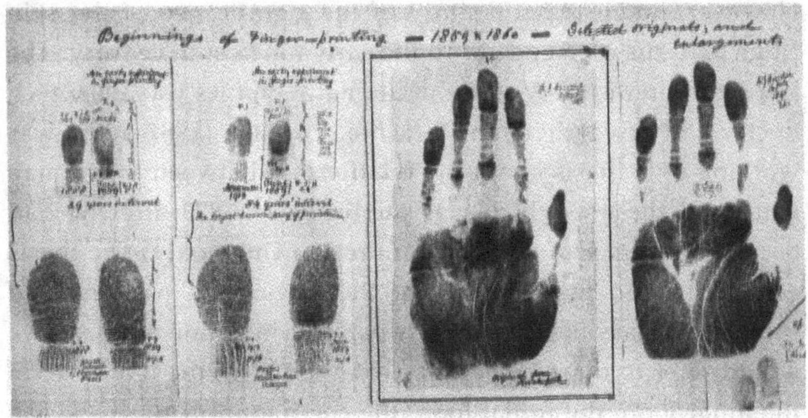

Herschel took his handprints in 1860 and 1890 to prove that the fingerprints don't change over time

In Argentina, **Juan Vucetich** had developed his own system of identification through the use of fingerprinting, and by 1891 this was being successfully employed by the Argentinian authorities. Although it was first suggested to the Home Office in 1887, it wasn't until 1901 that fingerprinting became an established procedure in criminological investigation in England. This came about largely through the efforts of Faulds and Herschel, in conjunction with Francis Galton.

Francis Galton (1822–1911), the cousin of Sir Charles Darwin, was a scientist with a wide range of interests covering anthropology, geology, biology, heredity and eugenics, publishing some 240 written works, including fifteen books. He conducted extensive research into the significance of skin ridge patterns, not only to demonstrate their permanence and consequently their use as a means of identification, but also to demonstrate the hereditary significance of fingerprints, and to show the biological variations of different fingerprint patterns amongst different ethnic groups. He collected vast numbers of fingerprints from all types of people, noting the variations of pattern types amongst different ethnicities and established

The Arch has no tri-radius

The Loop has one tri-radius

The Whorl has two tri-radii

the relative frequency with which each pattern type occurred amongst different peoples. His classification of fingerprint patterns was simpler than that proposed by Purkinje, delineating only three main types of patterns. He identified the triradius as being the significant indicator of a fingerprint pattern type and hence based his classification on the number of triradii to be found within each pattern.

The tri-radius is a small triangular-like formation in the skin ridges found adjacent to the pattern itself. Galton observed that in the three main types of fingerprint pattern, the arch had no triradius, the loop had one triradius, located to the side and the whorl had two triradii, one on either side of the spiral-shaped pattern that the whorl makes. This is a simple and straightforward method to assess and evaluate the different types of fingerprints that has been widely adopted in forensic investigation ever since. Although Galton recognises the other three patterns that can be found on the fingers, he subsumes them into this primary threefold classification and it is this system of classification rather than that of Purkinje which has been adopted by both the police and dermatoglyphicists, and this must be borne in mind when considering statistics from these sources.

However, Galton is perhaps the single most influential figure in the whole study of the skin ridge patterns of the hands and many of his methods for analysing fingerprints have carried through into the work of later genetic dermatoglyphic research. His two works *Fingerprints* (1892) and *Fingerprint Directories* (1895) are rightly considered as classics in the field of early dermatoglyphic research and stimulated the interest of all sorts of scientific investigators, from anthropologists and zoologists to geneticists and criminologists.

After Galton's initial pioneering work, many further investigations were undertaken to develop this fledgling science of fingerprint analysis, or "dermatoglyphics" as it became known. Anthropologists concentrated on researching dermatoglyphic distributions of different peoples from around the world, and work was done on clarifying both the methodology and morphology of dermatoglyphic analysis. Meanwhile, the scientific world pioneered studies to investigate the genetic significance of dermatoglyphic patterns and by the mid 1930s onwards, the hand was coming to be recognised as an important tool in the diagnosis of congenital syndromes such as Down Syndrome and other chromosomal disorders. This research was later extended to encompass all manner of diseases and conditions which have a genetic basis, including heart disease and cancer, such that the hand has been recognised as providing diagnostic clues for many diseases and conditions, from genetic disorders to systemic health issues seen in hand morphology, skin texture and fingernails.

Medical Dermatoglyphics

The main breakthrough in establishing the significance of the dermatoglyphic analysis of the hand came with the publication of the results of the research of Harold Cummins and Charles Midlo in their seminal work *Fingerprints, Palms and Soles* in 1943. Cummins and Midlo were professors of Microscopic Anatomy at Tulane University in the United States; they coined the term "dermatoglyphics" (*derma* = skin, *glyph* = carving) in 1926. The main thrust of their research was into Down Syndrome and its associated characteristic hand formations. They showed that the hand contained significant dermatoglyphic configurations that could assist in the identification of Down Syndrome in the new-born child. They also researched the embryogenesis of skin ridge patterns and established that the fingerprint patterns actually develop in the womb and are fully formed by the fourth foetal month.

Francis Galton (1822–1911)

Later, research was conducted into other disorders with a chromosomal basis, such as Edwards Syndrome and Patau's Syndrome as well as other very rare chromosomal disorders such as *Cri du Chat* Syndrome, and the sex chromosome disorders, Turner's Syndrome and Klinefelter's Syndrome. Much of this research was conducted by **LS Penrose** and his assistant **Sarah Holt** at the Kennedy-Galton Centre for Clinical Genetics and Mental Deficiency Research in Hertfordshire. The main thrust of scientific dermatoglyphic research in the latter half of the twentieth century was directed into genetic research and the diagnosis of chromosomal defects with many thousands of scientific papers having been written on the genetic significance of skin-ridge patterns. Whilst many of these have been restricted to the study of chromosomal disorders, significant investigations have also been carried out into the dermatoglyphic indicators of congenital heart disease, leukaemia, cancer, coeliac disease, intestinal disorders, rubella embryopathy, Alzheimer's disease, schizophrenia and other forms of mental illness. Most of this research has only been published in the pages of medical journals, but a good summary of these findings can be found in Schaumann and Alter's *Dermatoglyphics in Medical Disorders* published in 1976.

Noel Jaquin

One of the other most important pioneers in the field of dermatoglyphic analysis was the chirologist Noel Jaquin (1893–1974). Jaquin was the first to outline both the psychological and physiological significance of the different fingerprint pattern types in his book *The Signature of Time*, published in 1940. His assertions as to the physiological significance of the fingerprint patterns have since been amply confirmed by the research of dermatoglyphicists over the subsequent decades. More importantly, in his book *The Hand of Man* of 1933, he was the first to investigate the significance of the degeneration of skin-ridges in the palm and to correlate these with bacteriological infections of specific organs of the body. Jaquin's student, **Beryl Hutchinson MBE** (1891–1981) also made extensive investigations into the psychological significance of the dermatoglyphic patterns of the hand. She was the first person to outline the psychological significance of many of the palmar dermatoglyphic patterns in the hand. Her work of 1967 *Your Life in Your Hands* is seminal in this regard.

Noel Jaquin (1893–1974)[1]

Dermatoglyphic Terminology

Most dermatoglyphicists today follow the classification system developed by Francis Galton in the 1890s. According to Galton's system, the significant feature of the fingerprint pattern is the triangular pattern formed by the ridges coming together at a point, known as a tri-radius. The fingerprint patterns are then readily differentiated from one another by observing the number of triradii within the patterns. As we have seen, Galton classified fingerprint patterns into three types: the Arch, which has no triradius, the Loop, which has one triradius and the Whorl, which has two triradii.

Radial Loop on the Index finger and Ulnar Loop on the Middle finger

The loop fingerprint pattern is then sub-classified by Galton into the Ulnar loop and the Radial loop, according to the location of the triradius. In the Ulnar loop the triradius is on the Thumb side of the print and in the Radial loop, the triradius is on the Little finger side of the print pattern. The majority of dermatoglyphicists work with this Four-fold classification system of the fingerprints:

Arch, Whorl, Ulnar Loop and Radial Loop. The merits of this system are its simplicity and its ease of objective identification; in cases of composite or hybrid patterns, it is easy to determine the type of pattern simply by counting the number of triradii.

However, there is a significant issue with this classification system in that there are several other important pattern types which this classification overlooks. This includes the Tented Arch, the Double Loop (or Composite) and the Compound (or Peacock's Eye) fingerprints. Using Galton's system of counting the number of triradii to classify the pattern types, the Tented Arch is counted as a loop and the Double Loop and Compound patterns, given that they have two triradii, are classified as variations on the whorl. Chirological experience has shown that these are significant patterns and deserve to be considered as distinct patterns in their own right. Indeed, some dermatoglyphic researchers have differentiated these patterns and found them to be of both medical and genetic significance.

If we include these minor fingerprint patterns, it becomes evident that there are actually seven distinct fingerprint patterns. We need to have a **Seven-fold Classification System** to clearly differentiate the primary variations in the fingerprints.

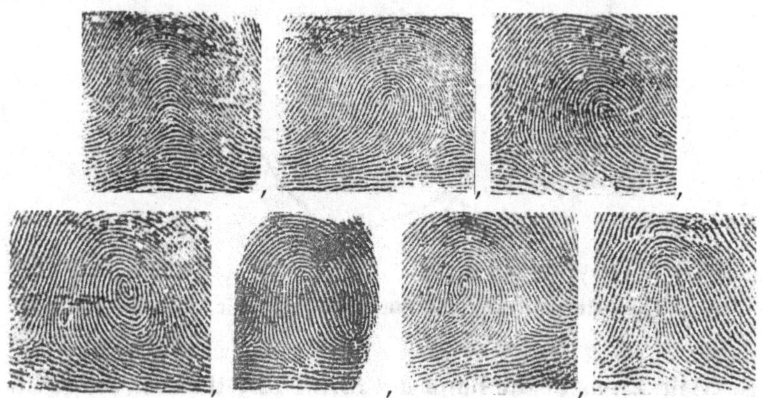

Illustrations of the seven main fingerprint patterns from Galton F "Fingerprint Directories" 1895

Palmar Considerations

The skin ridges that make up the fingerprints actually cover the entire surface of the palm; the triradius formation can also be seen in the palm. Usually, there are five triradii, one under each of the fingers and one located centrally at the base of the palm. In medical dermatoglyphic terminology, the digital triradii are labelled A-B-C-D from the Index finger to the Little finger and the triradius at the base of the palm, also known as the axial triradius, is labelled T.

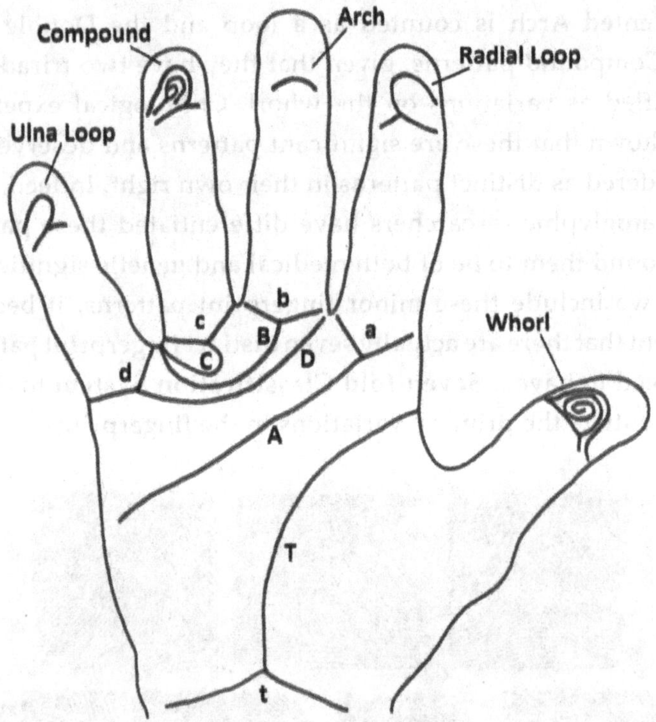

The palmar triradii and the dermatoglyphic Main Lines

The Main Lines of the hand are formed by the skin ridge lines which emanate from the apices of the triradii. These are usually drawn onto the imprint of the hand to trace the movement of the ridges across the surface of the palm. Each of the main lines has a typical ending and deviations from these normal endings have been noted to be significant in certain chromosomal disorders.

- The main line from the A triradius usually passes across the palm to the ulnar edge.
- The main line from the T triradius usually moves up the hand to end on the radial edge of the palm.
- The main lines from the other three triradii usually end within the confines of the three Interdigital areas at the base of the fingers.

The configuration of the main lines and their direction across the palm are obviously affected by the presence of patterns in the palm such as loops or whorls. In particular, the configuration of the main lines radiating from the b, c and d triradii are responsible for creating those loops that can be found between the fingers, called interdigital loops.

The palmar area is divided into three main areas, the hypothenar area on the ulnar side of the hand (below the little finger) and the thenar area (below the thumb) on the radial side of the hand and the interdigital area under the fingers. Specific palmar dermatoglyphic patterns such as loops are most commonly found in the hypothenar area but not often seen in the thenar area. The four Interdigital areas are identified and labelled as I^1, I^2, I^3 and I^4 from the Thumb out to the Little finger. Patterns are quite common in the I^3 and I^4 areas but rare in the I^1 and I^2 areas. This scientific description is frequently confirmed in chirological experience; the two most common palmar dermatoglyphic patterns are found between the middle and ring fingers and between the ring and little fingers.

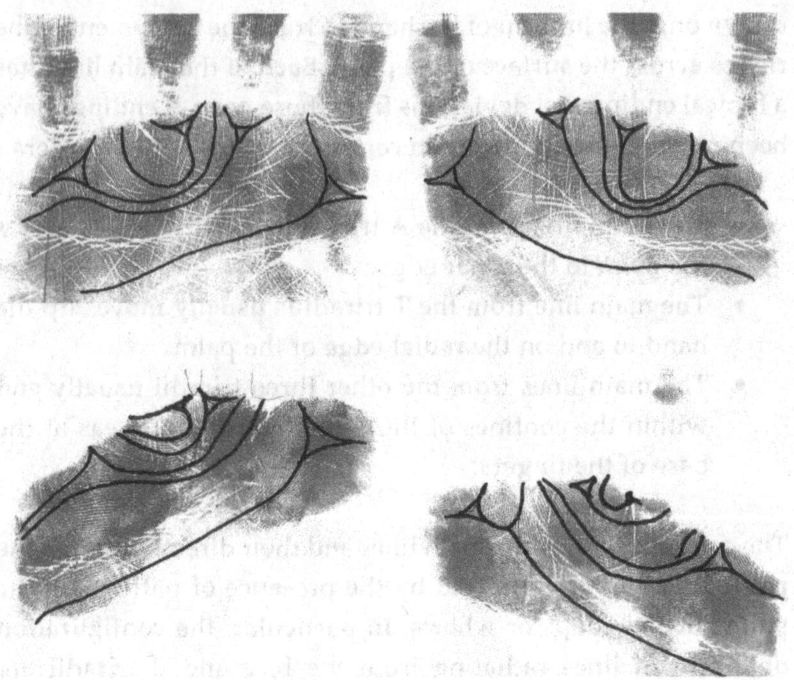

Interdigital ridge line variations

The ATD Angle

Identifying and measuring the ATD angle is a technique developed by LS Penrose to give a quantitative means of identifying the location of the axial triradius. The axial triradius is not usually missing from the hand but can at times be quite dramatically displaced from its usual location at the base of the palm.

The ATD angle is formed by drawing straight lines to connect triradius T with the triradii A and D. It is used to designate a triradius in its normal position at the base of the palm. This gives an ATD angle of about forty-five degrees.

t^1 is used to designate an ATD angle of between forty-five and fifty-seven degrees, whilst t^2 is used to designate an axial triradius which is so distally displaced it gives an ATD angle greater than fifty-seven degrees. Some lateral displacement of

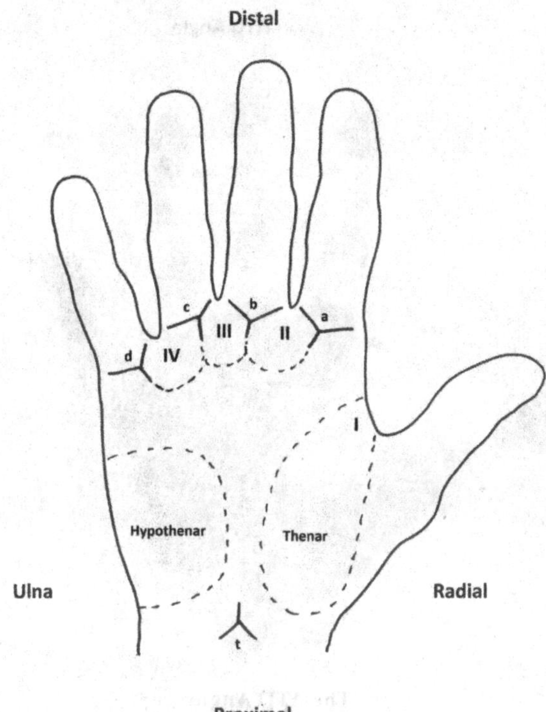

Palmar dermatoglyphic nomenclature

the axial triradius can also sometimes occur. This is designated by t^u or t^r according to whether the triradius is displaced towards the ulnar or radial side of the hand.

Penrose originally developed this technique to locate the exact position of the t triradius to differentiate between the palmar dermatoglyphics of Down Syndrome babies and chromosomally normal babies. He noticed that the axial triradius is very often displaced to a t^2 or even a t^3 position in the hands of those suffering from Down Syndrome. This is usually caused by the presence of palmar dermatoglyphic patterns in the hypothenar area, which is very common in the hands of people with Down Syndrome. The example here is, in fact, the hand of a Down Syndrome person. In addition, Penrose's research into the

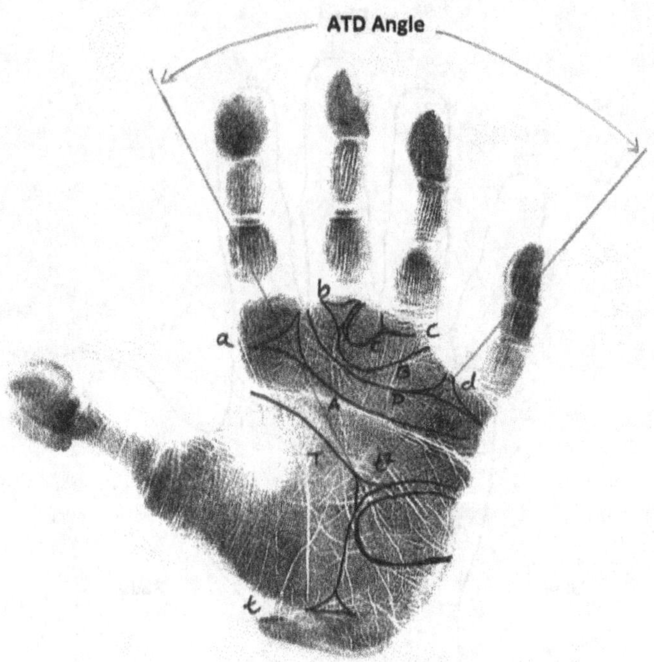

The ATD Angle

hands of parents of children with Down Syndrome proved that the location of this triradius is genetically inherited and that the presence of this displacement of the t triradius in the hand of the mother is an important indicator that she may be more likely to produce a child with Down Syndrome. Subsequent dermatoglyphic research has found the displaced axial triradius to be very common in other chromosomal abnormalities and also in certain forms of congenital heart disease. Scientifically considered, it is a very significant dermatoglyphic marker.

Anthropological Dermatoglyphic Studies

Right from the beginning of the scientific investigation into dermatoglyphics it was recognised that the fingerprint patterns could be of considerable anthropological significance. Galton proposed that different fingerprint patterns might occur in different distributions amongst different peoples and conducted the first studies to investigate this. It soon became clear that the different dermatoglyphic patterns cannot be specifically correlated with different cultures – all the pattern types occur in the hands of all peoples from around the world.

However, it also became evident that there is considerable variation in the distribution of fingerprint patterns in different parts of the world. Galton's preliminary studies found a greater incidence of Whorls in the peoples of the Pacific and Australasia and a greater incidence of Arches amongst the African populations that he studied, as compared to the hands of English Caucasians. Galton's work inspired a whole generation of anthropologists to investigate the fingerprint patterns of peoples from around the world and as a result we now have a vast body of information about the incidence of different fingerprint patterns in different parts of the world. Anthropologists have asserted that dermatoglyphic configurations are useful morphological phenomena in the anthropological study of different peoples and ethnicities.

Before considering these findings in detail, we should remind ourselves that most anthropological researchers have employed Galton's system of fingerprint classification. As we have seen, this distinguishes only four types of fingerprint pattern, the Arch, the Whorl, the Ulnar Loop and the Radial Loop. Double Loops and Compounds tend to be classified as Whorls and Tented Arches are usually classified as Loops – though Galton himself tended to classify Tented Arches along with Arches! The lack of differentiation of these last three pattern types should always be borne in mind when considering statistics on dermatoglyphic distributions from scientific or forensic sources.

More Whorls Less Arches

Galton's first studies of the fingerprints of English people formed the basis for all later dermatoglyphic comparative studies. He found the following distribution of fingerprint patterns in the UK population: Arches: 6.5% Whorls: 26.0% Loops: 67.5%, thereby showing that Loops are the dominant fingerprint pattern type by a very large margin. Later studies have confirmed that in fact the Loop pattern is the predominant fingerprint pattern type in nearly all ethnicities.

Naturally enough, this has prompted anthropologists to find a greater significance in the distribution of Whorls and Arches. In fact, it has now been established that there is an inverse proportional relationship between the number of Whorls and Arches; the more Arches there are, the less Whorls will be found and, equally, the more Whorls there are, the less Arches there will be. This is graphically illustrated by looking at the dermatoglyphic distributions of the Chinese and Japanese, who have a very high incidence of Whorls. In Chinese and Japanese peoples, Whorls occur on something like 45–50% of all digits whereas Arches only occur on 1–2.5% of all digits.

The inverse is true for those populations who evidence a greater number of Arches, such as certain groups of Europeans, Africans and other indigenous peoples, who have a corresponding decrease in the number of Whorls. The following statistics are drawn from Dankmeijer's article on *Anthropological Data on Dermatoglyphics* published in 1938[1]:

Population	Sample Size	Arch	Radial Loop	Ulna Loop	Whorl
Chinese	300	1.4%	2.7%	45.0%	50.7%
Japanese	285	1.1%	3.7%	47.3%	48.0%
Japanese	12,940	1.2%	3.9%	44.9%	50.1%
Koreans	700	2.6%	3.2%	48.7%	45.2%
Jews (New Orleans)	200	4.2%	3.0%	50.0%	42.7%
French	15,000	4.2%	66%		29.3%
Italians	1,579	4.7%	4.4%	54.0%	36.9%
Chileans	61,545	4.8%	4.4%	54.5%	36.3%
Hungarians	833	5.0%	3.6%	59.1%	32.3%
Germans	5,000	5.4%	5.1%	59.6%	29.8%
Danes (male)	86,654	5.4%	5.5%	59.3%	29.8%
Danes (female)	14,857	7.5%	4.4%	61.9%	26.2%
Norwegians	24,518	7.4%	5.8%	61.1%	25.7%
Dutch (males)	2,222	7.7%	5.4%	60.7%	26.2%
Dutch (females)	278	9.6%	3.7%	63.5%	23.2%
Mulattoes (Jamaica)	213	9.5%	2.8%	63.0%	24.7%
Efe Pygmies (Congo)	207	16.2%	2.7%	61.3%	19.6%

As can be seen from the table above, as the percentage of Arches increases, the percentage of Whorls decreases. A 1965 study of the hands of the Maori people of New Zealand found a very high incidence of Whorl fingerprint patterns – and a correspondingly low incidence of Arch patterns, with Whorls at around 63–68% and Arches at less than 1%[2]:

Maori Males: Whorls=68.77%; Loops=30.77%; Arches=0.46% (n=430)

Maori Females: Whorls=63.47%; Loops=35.89%; Arches=0.64% (n=236)

The highest incidence of Whorls ever to have been found was amongst the Inuit populations of Greenland. Although only a small sample was taken, 72.2% of the digits were found to have Whorls and only 0.8% of the digits were found to have Arches.

The highest incidence of Arches ever to have been found was amongst the Efe Pygmies of what was the Belgian Congo in Africa. Here 16.2% of digits were found to have Arches whereas only 19.6% of digits had Whorls. Despite the abundance of

Arches, note that the Loop was still the dominant pattern overall. The Ulnar Loop is the dominant fingerprint pattern in the majority of the world's ethnic populations.

Gender Differences

An important differentiation in the dermatoglyphic distributions in males and females was also noted fairly early on in anthropological dermatoglyphic research. It was found that men tend to have a greater incidence of Whorls whilst women tend to have a greater incidence of Arches. Holt gives the following distributions based on a sample of 1,000 English people:

Males: **Whorls=28% Ulnar Loops=62%**
Radial Loops=6% Arches=4.3%

Females: **Whorls=24% Ulnar Loops=66%**
Radial Loops=5% Arches=5.7%

What is quite remarkable is that this gender-based pattern of distribution holds for all peoples. Regardless of the overall abundance of Whorls or Arches in any given population, Whorls are less commonly found on women and Arches are less commonly found on men. The Danish sample in the above table also shows that same gender-based distribution of fingerprint patterns.

In addition, the two Loop patterns also show a gender bias for all peoples; the Ulnar Loop is more common in women whilst the Radial Loop is more common in men. Samples of dermatoglyphic distributions need to be collected separately for the males and females of a population if accurate dermatoglyphic comparisons are to be made.

Other Dermatoglyphic Discoveries

All kinds of other interesting discoveries have been made in the course of the investigations into the distribution of dermatoglyphics in the hand. Some of the more relevant data is given below, based on samples from English populations gathered by Holt and Penrose and Scotland Yard.

- Arch fingerprints occur more frequently in the left hand whilst Whorls occur more frequently in the right hand.
- Interdigital Loop patterns are found more commonly in the I^4 position in the left hand but more commonly in the I^3 position in the right hand.
- There is an inverse relationship between the I^3 and I^4 patterns such that if the one is found in a hand, then it is unlikely to find the other.
- The I^2 pattern placement is the rarest of the three Interdigital Loops but has been found to be more common on the right hand than the left.
- Ten Whorls on the fingers occurs in about 3% of people i.e. about 1/35 people.
- Ten Loops on the fingers occurs in about 4% of people i.e. about 1/25 people.
- Ten Arches occur much more rarely – only about 0.1% normal males (1/1000) have ten Arches whereas about 0.4% females (1/250) have ten Arches.

---

1. Dankmeijer J *Anthropological data on dermatoglyphics* Am J Phys Anthr v23 1938
2. Veale & Adams *Finger-Prints of the New Zealand Maori* Journal of the Anthropological Society of Nippon 1965 Volume 73 also accessible at: https://www.jstage.jst.go.jp/article/ase1911/73/2/73_2_33/_article

Variant Fingerprint Patterns

Sometimes **Arches** can take on the appearance of a Loop, but unless there is a recurving ridge line then it is definitely an Arch. Conversely, some **Loops** can be low-lying and look more like an Arch – but if there is a recurving ridge line – a ridge line that goes back from whence it came, then it is definitely a Loop.

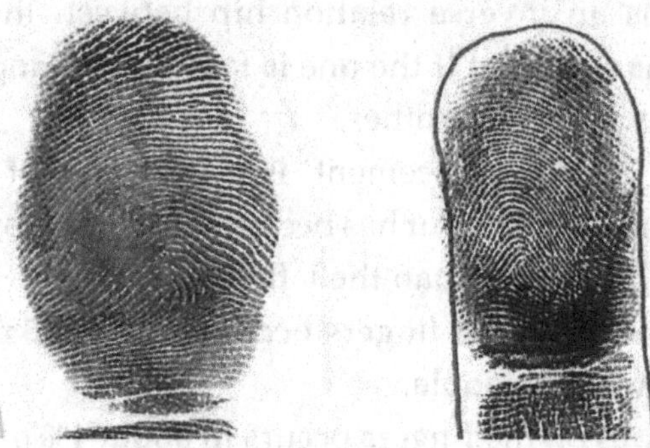

Examples of low-lying loops

Tented Arches can be high thrusting spikes or much smaller angled points. But in all cases the triradius is centrally located *and there are no recurving ridges* as that would make it into a Loop.

Examples of Tented Arches

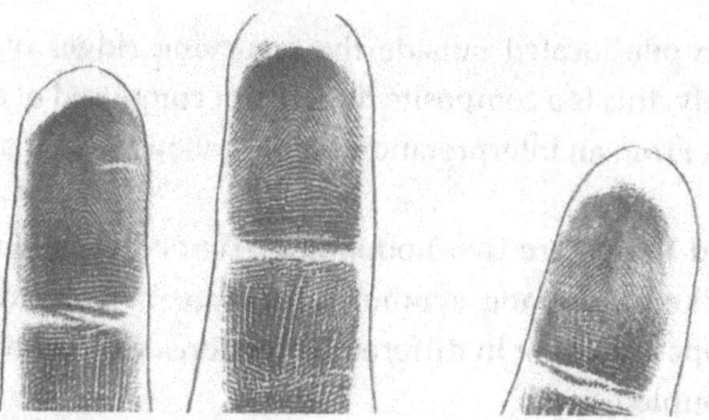

Variations on Arches that are not Tented Arches

A **Nutant Loop** is a variant Loop where it comes in from the side and "flops" over. It's a very rare pattern – rarer than Composites and Accidentals so striking when seen. Malcom X had one on his Thumb. Check whether it is an Ulnar or Radial Loop and interpret accordingly.

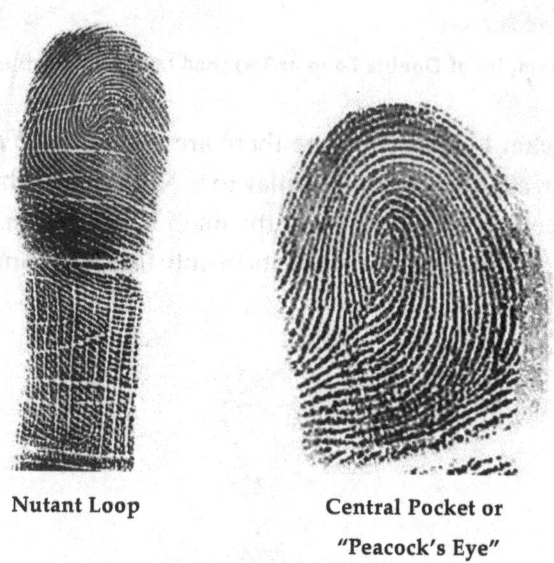

Nutant Loop

Central Pocket or "Peacock's Eye"

Central Pockets or Compounds are Loops with a Whorl in the centre. They look like a tail feather of a peacock, hence the common name of a Peacock's Eye. There are two triradii, one by the core and then one located outside the recurving ridges of the Loop. Effectively, this is a composite fingerprint composed of a Loop and a Whorl. From an interpretation point of view, treat it as a Whorl.

Twinned Loops are two Loops inter-twined together and look rather like a yin-yang symbol. There are two triradii and the two Loops are going in different directions. Commonly referred to as Double Loops.

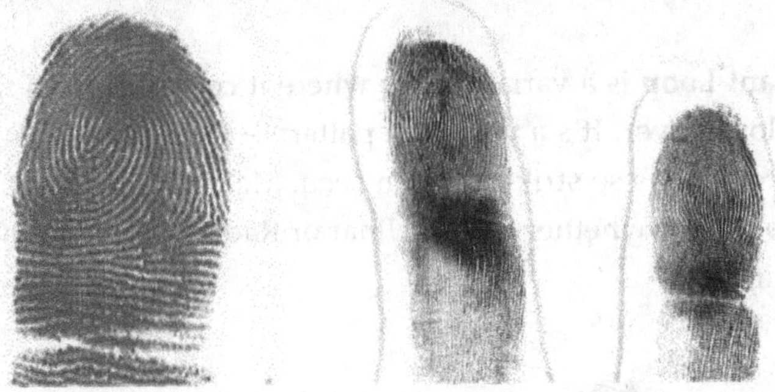

Examples of Double Loop or Twinned Loop fingerprints

Lateral Pocket Loops are where there are two Loops, *but going in the same direction*. They look similar to a Nutant Loop but have a smaller second Loop underneath the main Loop pattern. Scotland Yard have discovered these variants in only 0.154% of fingerprints.

Lateral Pocket Loop

Composites and Accidentals are two different names given to other rare and random formations of fingerprints which can have 3 or 4 triradii and can sometimes look like a malformed Whorl. Any unusual pattern is just that, it shows something unusual. According to statistics from Scotland Yard, Composites are found in 0.162% of fingerprints and Accidentals in only 0.046% of fingerprints, so they are *very* rare. Standard Whorls are idiosyncratic enough already – these are more idiosyncratic again!

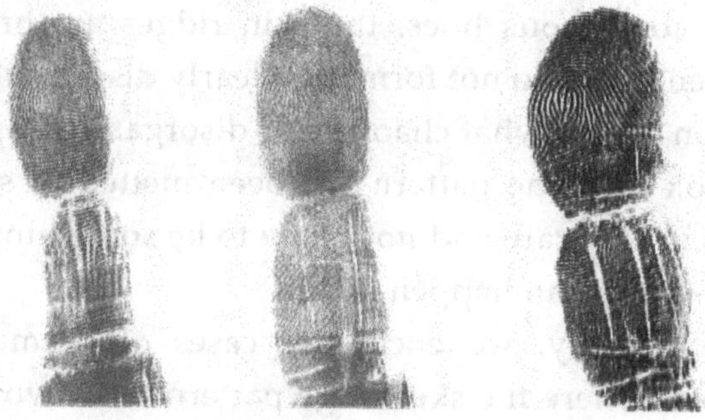

Composite and Accidental fingerprints

Dermatoglyphic Malformations

Usually, the skin ridge patterns of the palm are well-formed and clearly defined and the majority of fingerprint patterns are also usually very easy to classify, with 99% of all fingerprints coming under one of the seven main types of patterns. Occasionally, patterns are found which cannot easily be classified, but these generally tend to be patterns which are composite configurations of other types of fingerprints.

Aplasia

Very occasionally, we find fingerprints that are very hard to discern. There is an extremely rare congenital malformation of the dermatoglyphics called aplasia or *adermatoglyphia* of the skin ridges where there is a complete absence of the ridges on the surfaces of the palms of the hands and the soles of the feet. Instead, the skin is smooth and parchment-like and has the appearance of the skin on the back of the hand, but without hair. In this era of biometric identification, the absence of fingerprints can have extremely annoying consequences – adermatoglyphia is also known as "immigration delay disease"!

Dysplasia

Dysplasia of the skin ridge patterns is another congenital dermatoglyphic malformation. Here, rather than being arranged in smooth, continuous lines, the skin ridges are broken into short segments and do not form any clearly discernible pattern. They take on a somewhat chaotic and disorganised appearance and can look as if the pattern has been melted in some way. Again, this is very rare and not likely to be something you will encounter – but it can happen.

More commonly, we encounter cases of dermatoglyphic deterioration, where the skin ridge patterns are "worn down", almost to the point of being invisible. This is common in the hands of older people, where it is caused by the thinning of the skin due to ageing. However, it can also be seen in the hands of those who handle rough objects, such as manual workers or rock climbers and in the hands of those whose occupation involves the continual immersion of the hands in liquids and cleaning agents. In these cases, the skin ridge deterioration is evidently caused by the wearing down of the skin, and these changes are readily reversible if the causes are removed.

White Lines

The fingerprints can also sometimes become obscured by line formations, sometimes to the point of making the fingerprint patterns almost invisible. This is generally an indication of psychological stress, if the lines are horizontally placed, but may also point to neurological agitation or even endocrinological imbalance if the lineation is vertically or longitudinally aligned on the phalange.

Ridges Off the End Syndrome

Another interesting and very rare congenital dermatoglyphic anomaly is the formation known as "ridges off the end syndrome" (ROES). Instead of the usual alignment of the skin ridges in the fingerprint patterns, where they curve round as they near the distal end of the finger, the ridges are aligned in more of a straight line and run directly off the edge of the fingertip.

At first glance, this configuration resembles the Tented Arch pattern, given that both share a centrally located triradius. But on closer inspection it can be seen that the ridges do not fold over the triradius as they do in the Tented Arch. In addition, sometimes a second triradius formation occurs right at the tip of the finger itself! This unusual dermatoglyphic configuration was first noticed in 1933, and later described by Cherrill (1954) as "non-descript freak patterns".

The term *Ridges Off the End Syndrome* was coined by TJ David in 1971, in a paper he gave to demonstrate the genetic inheritance of fingerprint patterns.[1] In one family he studied, ten out of eighteen family members, over three generations, had ROES fingerprints. Given their extreme rarity, it is unlikely that such a cluster of this strange dermatoglyphic anomaly would occur by any mechanism other than genetics.

Whilst his studies confirmed the genetic inheritance of fingerprints, he did not find this pattern had any particular negative medical or genetic significance. None of those with this pattern had suffered any major serious ailments nor had any congenital conditions. Indeed, David noted that all those with this pattern were remarkably free of serious disease. However, he did suggest that this pattern may give some form of genetic immunity to diseases due to atherosclerosis, such

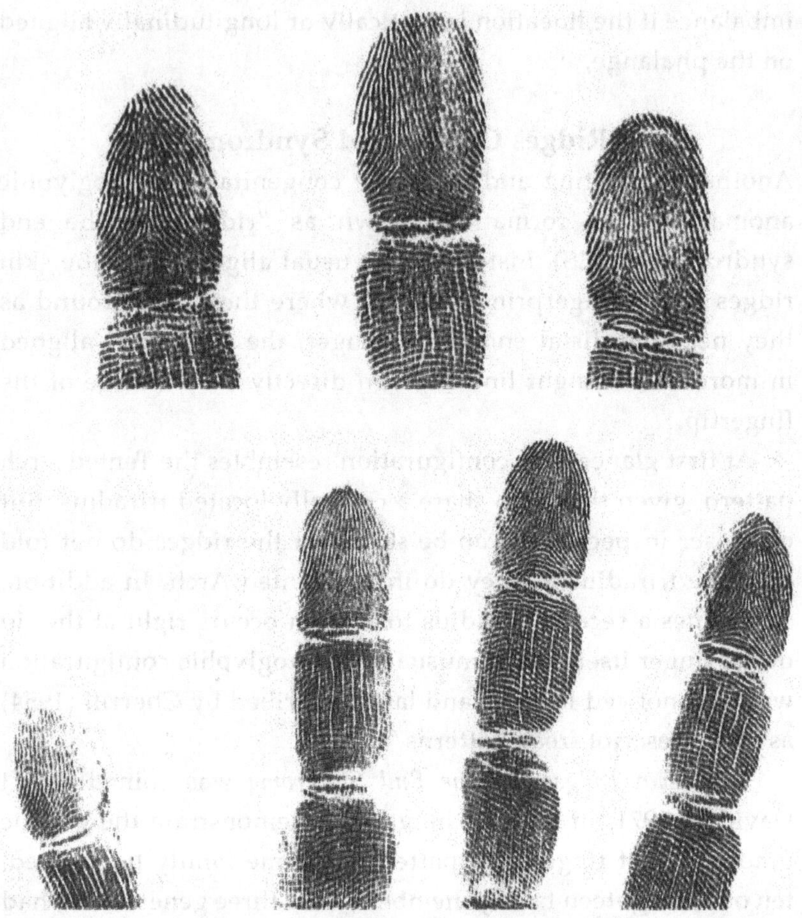

Fingerprints in Ridges off the End Syndrome

as heart attacks and strokes, though he admitted that more research needed to be done to confirm this with certainty; there does not appear to have been any other studies done on ROES over the last 50 years.

The similarity in formation of the ROES pattern to the Tented Arch-type fingerprint suggests that the significance of this formation may be related more to that of the Tented Arch itself. Given that the Tented Arch relates to the nervous system and can indicate a nervous, sensitive or highly strung disposition, even when found singly, we might expect this disposition to be proportionally more marked in cases of people with ROES. For, whereas the Tented Arch is rare on the fingers, it seems that when the ROES pattern occurs, it is usually found on six to ten of the digits.

In the one case that I have encountered illustrated above, this was indeed the case, for the subject did show a marked hyperactivity of mind and verbal effusiveness. This nervous hyperactivity also manifested temperamentally as a distinct dissipation of her energy, something which is perhaps suggested by the unbounded nature of the fingerprints themselves.

---

1. David TJ *Ridges off the End – A Dermatoglyphic Syndrome* Human Heredity v21 1971; David TJ *Ridge Dissociation & R.O.E.S.* Human Heredity v23 1973; David TJ *Congenital Malformations of human dermatoglyphs* Arch Dis Child v48 1973

Digital Dermatoglyphic Distributions

Most of the statistical studies on dermatoglyphic distributions work with the classification system set out by Francis Galton or the Henry System, as used by the UK police at Scotland Yard. Many of the charts reproduced by various authors therefore only record the distributions of three of the major dermatoglyphic patterns found in the hands of a select sample of people, the Loop the Whorl and the Arch. Much of the statistical work on dermatoglyphics, notwithstanding studies of those with chromosomal abnormalities, has therefore almost necessarily been based upon surveys of criminal hands, rather than from a wider cross-section of the community. In a sense, this is unsurprising, since the general acceptance of fingerprinting as a means of identification and its subsequent use by police forces around the world has made criminal groups the largest source of dermatoglyphic imprints. However, it is obvious that what may be true of the criminal population may not be true of the population as a whole.

In 1991, I conducted research into the distribution of dermatoglyphic patterns on the fingers, using my own collection of hand imprints. Whilst the sample is much smaller than the surveys from Scotland Yard (10,000 hands in 1905 and 20,000 hands in 1954), it is taken from a wide cross-section of the UK population, none of whom to my knowledge had any criminal orientation.

From that study, I found it necessary to discriminate at least *seven* different dermatoglyphic patterns. In addition to the **Arch**, the **Whorl**, the **Ulnar Loop** and the **Radial Loop**, I consider it important to distinguish also the **Tented Arch**, the **Double Loop** and the **Compound /Peacock's Eye** as distinct patterns. Galton's classification is too simplistic, so it seems better justified to follow the original classificatory scheme suggested by Purkinje back in 1823, albeit modifying his scheme a little to bring all the different types of whorls together. There are some other variant patterns, but these occur so infrequently (less than 0.5%) that I have not characterized them.

In practice, it is important to distinguish these three other minor dermatoglyphic patterns, given their relative frequency. For instance, a Compound on the Ring finger or a Double Loop on the Thumb are both more commonly found than a Whorl on the Little finger.

In addition, it is important to note that in most scientific and forensic statistical compilations, the Tented Arches were classified as Loops (since a Tented Arch only has one triradius) whilst the Double Loop was classed as a Whorl, it being perceived as having two triradii. However, the patterns are sufficiently distinct, both in form and in psychological significance, to merit separate classification.

Given these slight differences in classification and in the type of persons involved in the samples, it is interesting to compare the frequency charts of dermatoglyphic distributions. What can be observed is that even though the exact percentages vary slightly, the pattern of my smaller survey echoes the patterns of the larger collection of statistics. The Scotland Yard statistics found Whorls to occur marginally more frequently in their samples than amongst the general population but not enough to justify their assertion that the whorl is associated with being a sign of criminal tendencies! Rather than classify a many-whorled hand as being a criminal hand, it is important to understand not only the psychological significance of the pattern itself, but also, to take all other features of the hand into consideration. As I shall show in a later book, the criminal hand is not most readily characterised by Whorl fingerprint patterns at all.

The Oxford Dermatoglyphic Study

This study was conducted in 1991 on a sample of 500 handprints from my own personal collection and, whilst small, nonetheless reflects the larger sample sizes collected by the UK Police at Scotland Yard. All these samples are representative of a

Caucasian UK population. For the details of the findings of these studies, see Appendix One.

I found that the seven main fingerprint patterns were distributed in the following percentages:

Major Dermatoglyphs			Minor Dermatoglyphs		
Ulnar Loops	1449	= 58.0%	Radial Loops	121	= 4.8%
Whorls	493	= 19.7%	Double Loops	106	= 4.2%
Arches	203	= 8.1%	Peacock's Eye	93	= 3.7%
			Tented Arch	26	= 1.0%
			Other	9	= 0.4%

What becomes clear from this survey is that the seven main fingerprint pattern types account for over 99.5% of all fingerprint patterns encountered, confirming the value and sufficiency of this fingerprint classification system.

The Seven Main Fingerprint Patterns

As can readily be seen, the Ulnar Loop pattern is clearly the most dominant pattern to be found, occurring more frequently than all the other patterns put together. The Tented Arch is the rarest of all patterns, occurring on only 1% of all digits examined.

It is quite common for a hand to be Loop-dominated or Whorl-dominated and, occasionally, one finds an Arch-dominated hand. Of the 250 persons examined:

114 had seven or more Ulnar Loops (45.6%) – about 1 in 2 people

25 had seven or more Whorls (10%) – about 1 in 10 people

7 had seven or more Arches (2.8%) – about 1 in 35 people

These follow the relative frequency of each of the main patterns. Given that less than 3% of the samples were Arch-dominant, one would not expect to find a hand dominated by any of the minor dermatoglyphs. In any case, this would be extremely unusual.

Most Common

Each of the main fingerprint patterns has a digit upon which it is found more commonly:

Ulnar Loop – on the Little finger (80.2%) 4 in 5 persons
Whorl – on the Ring finger (30.8%) 1 in 3
Arch – on the Index finger (13.6%) 1 in 8
Radial Loop – on the Index finger (20.4%) 1 in 5
Double Loop – on the Thumb (11.2%) 1 in 9
Peacock's Eye – on the Ring finger (10.8%) 1 in 10
Tented Arch – on the Index finger (4.0%) 1 in 25

Which is to say, if we are going to find a particular fingerprint, this list shows where we would expect to see that fingerprint. It is important to know, therefore, upon which fingers it is *unusual* to find a particular fingerprint, for the rarer the placement the more significant it will be in the life of the person.

Most Rare

Equally, each of the main fingerprint patterns has a digit upon which it is found more rarely:

Ulnar Loop – on the Index finger (30.2%) 1 in 3
Whorl – on the Little finger (10.6%) 1 in 10
Arch – on the Little finger (3.4%) 1 in 32
Double Loop – on the Ring finger (0.8%) 1 in 125
Radial Loop – on the Little finger (0%)
Tented Arch – on the Little finger and Thumb (0%)

The research of Beryl Hutchinson[1] gives some support to the pattern of fingerprint distributions that I have found here. She too finds the Ulnar Loop to be the most common pattern, particularly on the Little finger. Radial Loops occur most frequently on the Index finger, but rarely on the other digits. She too has never seen a Radial Loop on the Little finger. Whorls, she agrees, occur most frequently on the Ring finger, but are also common on the Index finger and Thumb.

Arches are uncommon on the Ring and Little fingers, except when part of an Arch-dominant hand.

Of the major dermatoglyphic patterns, she cites a greater incidence of Whorls (25% of all digits) than found in this study, and also a greater (unspecified) incidence of Arches on the Thumb and the Index finger. She finds the Arch pattern *frequently* on the Thumb and Index finger, whereas I have classed these occurrences as *occasional*.

Of the minor dermatoglyphs, she too finds the Double Loop most commonly on the Thumb, followed by the Index finger, and then more rarely on the other digits. She gives no estimates for the occurrence of the Compound on other digits but agrees that it occurs most frequently on the Ring finger. As to the Tented Arch, she concurs that it is found most frequently on the Index finger and that it is rare on other digits. She has only seen one example of the Tented Arch on either the Thumb or the Little finger, thus confirming the rarity of this pattern. She too has never seen a full set and considers 4/10 Tented Arches on the fingers to be a high count. In only one example did I see more than two Tented Arches in the hands.

I have divided the dermatoglyphic distribution on the digits into four categories based on the percentages in which they occurred. More than about 20% occurrence classed the pattern as Common; between 5% and 15% classed the pattern as Occasional. Less than 5% occurrence makes the pattern Uncommon, whereas less than 2% makes the pattern (very) Rare. For the full details of the breakdown of the distribution of the fingerprints on each of the fingers, see Appendix One.

On the whole, we can see that the Ulnar Loop is indeed the most common dermatoglyphic pattern, followed by the Whorl, the Arch, the Radial Loop, the Double Loop, the Peacock's Eye and the Tented Arch. The Tented Arch is the rarest of all the main dermatoglyphic patterns.

The **Ulnar Loop** is most common on the Little (Air) finger, followed by Middle (Earth) finger, Thumb, Ring (Fire) finger, and is least common on the Index (Water) finger.

The **Whorl** is most common on the Ring (Fire) finger, followed by the Index (Water) finger, Thumb, Middle (Earth) finger and is least common on the Little (Air) finger.

The **Arch** is most common on the Index (Water) finger, followed by Middle (Earth) finger, Thumb, Ring (Fire) finger, and is least common on the Little (Air) finger.

The **Radial Loop** is most common on the Index (Water) finger, followed by Middle (Earth) finger, Ring (Fire) finger, Thumb and is least common on the Little (Air) finger.

The **Double Loop** is most common on the Thumb, followed by Index (Water) finger, Middle (Earth) finger, Little (Air) finger, and is least common on the Ring (Fire) finger.

The **Peacock's Eye** is most common on the Ring (Fire) finger, followed by Little (Air) finger, Index (Water) finger, Middle (Earth) finger, and is least common on the Thumb.

The **Tented Arch** is most common on the Index (Water) finger, followed by the Middle (Earth) finger, Ring (Fire) finger and is least common on the Thumb and Little (Air) finger.

It is as well to remember that though usefully comparable for many Caucasian populations, these fingerprint distributions are significant to the UK population and there may be some variations in the occurrence of fingerprints in different population samples, especially amongst non-European peoples. We await the results of further ethnological studies from Asian, African and Polynesian peoples to see how these distributions might differ.

---

1. Beryl Hutchinson *Your Life in Your Hands* (Sphere 1967) pp. 94–107

Table of Frequency of Occurrence of Dermatoglyphic Patterns on Digits

Digit	Dermatoglyphic	Status
Thumb	Ulnar Loop	Common
	Whorl	"
	Double Loop	Occasional
	Arch	"
	Peacock's Eye	*Very Rare*
	Radial Loop	*Very Rare*
	Tented Arch	*Never Seen*
Water	Ulnar Loop	Common
	Whorl	"
	Radial Loop	"
	Arch	Occasional
	Double Loop	Uncommon
	Tented Arch	"
	Peacock's Eye	*Very Rare*
Earth	Ulnar Loop	Common
	Arch	Occasional
	Whorl	"
	Double Loop	Uncommon
	Radial Loop	"
	Peacock's Eye	*Very Rare*
	Tented Arch	*Very Rare*
Fire	Ulnar Loop	Common
	Whorl	"
	Peacock's Eye	Occasional
	Arch	Uncommon
	Double Loop	*Very Rare*
	Radial Loop	*Very Rare*
	Tented Arch	*Very Rare*
Air	Ulnar Loop	Common
	Whorl	Occasional
	Peacock's Eye	Uncommon
	Arch	"
	Double Loop	*Very Rare*
	Radial Loop	*Never Seen*
	Tented Arch	*Never Seen*

Elemental Nomenclature

In order to understand the chirological approach to assessing the significance of fingerprint patterns it is useful to know the elemental names used within chirological handreading traditions. The four elements Earth, Water, Fire and Air are understood not just as a form of convenient nomenclature but are, rather, a *hermeneutic*. They are a key to unlock the mysteries of each person's uniqueness as shown by the features of the hands. We shall follow this elemental perspective as we uncover the significance of each of the fingerprints.

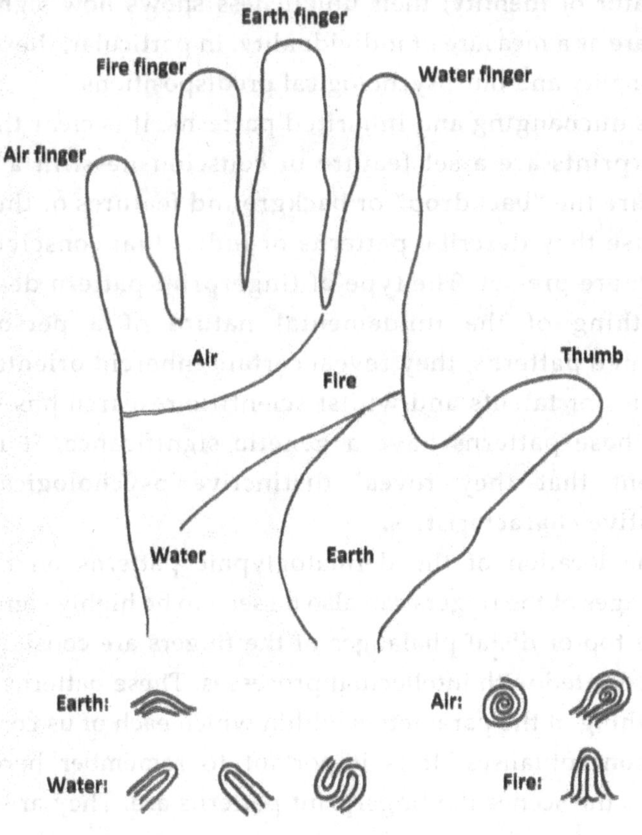

The Psychological Significance of Digital Dermatoglyphics

The dermatoglyphic (lit. "skin-carvings") patterns of the hand are the intimate and private symbols of the individual. Although this is true of all the skin-ridge patterns on the surface of the hand as a whole, it is especially true of the digital dermatoglyphs, the fingerprints. Everybody knows that we each possess a unique set of fingerprints, and moreover, that these patterns do not change, a fact which is put to much use by police forces around the world. Their use as a means of biometric identification shows how significant they are as an indicator of identity; their uniqueness shows how significant they are as a measure of individuality. In particular, they reveal personality and our psychological predispositions.

As unchanging and inherited patterns, it is clear that our fingerprints are a set feature of consciousness. In a sense, they are the "backdrop" or background features of the hand because they describe patterns of individual consciousness which are pre-set. The type of fingerprint pattern describes something of the fundamental nature of a person. As inherited patterns, they reveal certain inherent orientations, abilities or talents and whilst scientific research has shown that these patterns have a genetic significance, it is also evident that they reveal distinctive psychological and cognitive characteristics.

The location of the dermatoglyphic patterns on the top phalanges of the fingers can also be seen to be highly significant as the top or distal phalanges of the fingers are considered to be associated with intellectual processes. These patterns reveal something of the parameters within which each of us conceives and conceptualises. It is important to remember here how behind the scenes the fingerprint patterns are. They are not so much what we think, but *how* we think about what we think. They are so much a part of how we perceive and experience the world that we ordinarily assume that everyone thinks in the same way we do. But of course, this is not true and the differences that can be found between different people with regard to their fingerprint patterns reveals this.

However, even though we may share the same fingerprint pattern type as many other people, and hence share the same frame of reference, ultimately our psychological patterns are unique to us. Not even identical twins have identical fingerprint patterns! Our fingerprints therefore reveal something of our unique individuality. They form a crucial part of our individual identity and they thereby reveal both the style of our individuality and the manner in which this is expressed.

As we have already seen, there are seven main types of fingerprint patterns: the Ulnar Loop, the Whorl, the Arch, the Double Loop, the Radial Loop, the Peacock's Eye and the Tented Arch. These pattern types can be readily classified according to each of the four elements. The use of the elements enables us to understand the psychological significance of these patterns with greater clarity.

Earth Dermatoglyphic – the Arch

The fundamental motivations of the Arch are to provide protection and security for themselves and others, especially their family. These people are characterised by dedication, loyalty, commitment and a sense of responsibility, which in turn makes them steady, consistent and useful workers and citizens. Their desire for security can manifest itself as a desire for allegiance with others, whether as a family, a tribe, a group or a nation. There is a strong sense of support and solidarity. This desire for security can also create a certain caution and reserve. They can be reluctant to face change and can have difficulty responding to and adapting to new ideas and unexpected

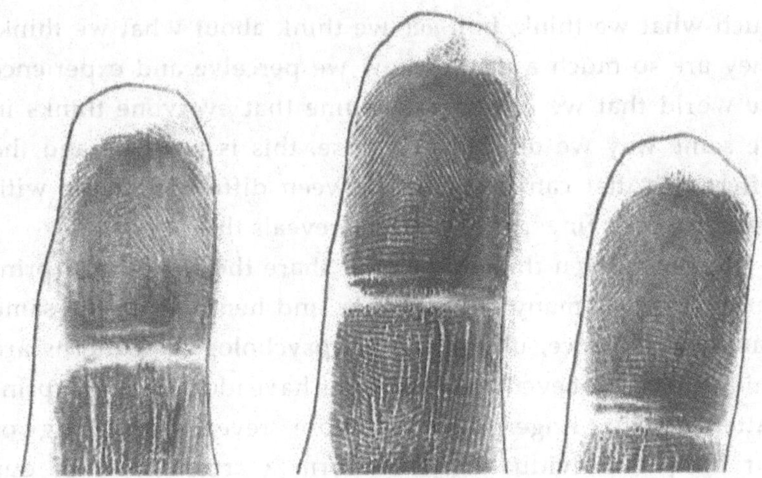

Arch fingerprints are ruled by Earth

circumstances. This resistance to change can manifest as defiant obstinacy and stubbornness. The Arch is naturally suspicious of anything until it has proven itself. The desire for security requires certainties, not doubt.

In terms of self-expression, the Arch is often self-repressive or self-abnegating. In part this is self-defence, but they tend to have a reserved rather than expressive nature. There can be difficulties in articulation which can either produce slowness of speech or a hesitant, almost stuttering form of speech. They like to be doing rather than thinking or talking. Most of all they can be inarticulate about their feelings, which they find difficult to express even to themselves, and so they can be somewhat emotionally inhibited particularly if this pattern is on the little finger. Putting others first is more important to them.

Above all else, the Arch gives practicality. They like to acquire practical and/or marketable skills by which they can make themselves useful to society and thereby gain the employment needed to have a certain material security. People with Arches often have a skilled pair of hands and an innate ability to make or repair things. Consequently, they often tend towards trades or professions which involve skilled manual work. The presence of many Arches on one hand can indicate the skilled specialist – someone who likes to have practical skills but has developed a speciality such as a traditional craftsman.

It is relatively rare to find an Arch-dominant hand. Contrary to what might be expected, people with many Arches are frequently actively rebellious in most of their activities, rebelling against conventions rather than abiding by them. They can be rather stubborn and defiant – the Arch-dominant person is as unconventional as she is uncommon.

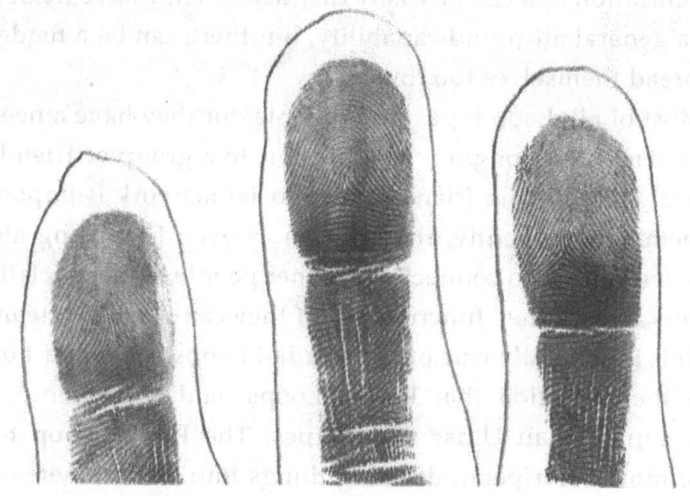

Loop fingerprints are ruled by Water

Water Dermatoglyphics – Ulnar and Radial Loops

The Loop pattern is the most common pattern to be found on the fingertips, and so we can deduce that the Loop pattern indicates a conventional, normal type of person. They tend to be group orientated and thus they mix well with others socially, and they are great team players. The Loop gives flexibility and adaptability; hence these are people who fit in well with others and are good at dealing with other people. In fact, the Loop is highly responsive to all things – new ideas, changing circumstances, the environment as well as to other people. But they tend to follow rather than to lead, to blend with the crowd rather than stand out from it, consequently, there tends to be a lack of individualism here and a tendency to conform.

Mentally, Loops reveal a versatile and assimilative mind. Loops being of the water element can be imaginative and can have a strong aesthetic appreciation, because they have a highly receptive and impressionable mind. However, sometimes they are too easily impressed, which can lead to gullibility. A predominance of Loops reveals a mind that can lack concentration and can be easily distracted. They have flexibility and a general all-round capability, but there can be a tendency to spread themselves too thinly.

Most of all, Loop types need people, for they have a need to feel a sense of belonging, whether it is to a group of friends or a social club: having friends and a social network is important to them. Consequently, they dislike or even fear being alone. They feel a need to connect with other people, either socially or at work, where they function best if they can work in a team.

This is generally true of both Radial Loops and Ulnar Loops, with the exception that Radial Loops tend to be more self-preoccupied than Ulnar Loop types. The Radial Loop tends to be more centripetal, drawing things into itself, whereas the Ulnar Loop tends to be more centrifugal and hence more able to accommodate others. However, the Ulnar Loop person more often has a clearer idea of themselves, as their expression of individuality comes from within them rather than from external influences. This can readily be seen by reference to the direction in which each of these different Loops point on the hand itself. The Radial, though more self-assertive, tends to internalise the external environment; the Ulnar, though more passive and receptive, tends to externalise themselves. The ramifications of these different types of Loop pattern will be considered more fully when we look at each of the fingerprint pattern types on each of the different fingers. Although the Ulnar Loop is extremely common on all digits, the Radial Loop is only commonly found on the Index finger and it is there that this pattern has its greatest significance.

Water Dermatoglyphics – Double Loop

In this pattern we have two Loops going in two directions. The most common manifestation of the Double Loop is one of duality of thought, which most often creates inner conflict, confusion and self-mistrust. The area of life which the Double Loop rules, as indicated by the digit on which it is found, will reveal the area of life where the individual experiences most confusion and conflict. Everything they do here is undermined by self-doubt and questioning. They frequently have regrets and wish they had done something else other than that which they did.

The Double Loop pattern enables them to see the value of various alternatives or the merits of both sides of an argument. As a result they can be incredibly indecisive, finding they are pulled equally in two or more directions and often cannot choose between them. Uncertainty and vacillation are common features of their experience, and they commonly get in a muddle. For example, the conflict of choices can manifest as a continual battle between material/practical considerations getting the better of their more idealistic aspirations. Consequently, they can often defeat their own attempts to achieve their goals or desires. Because their aspirations are undermined by self-doubt,

Double Loop

defeatist attitudes can settle in, and they may be prone to give up too easily. Continual encouragement from others to persist in the pursuit of their ideals may prove fruitful.

We can't change our dermatoglyphic patterns so rather than fight them or be defeated by them, we can come to terms with them and work with them. Double Loops need to come to terms with the cyclical and dual nature of their experience. Emotionally, they tend to experience considerable highs and lows and can be subject to mood swings. Rather than being depressed by the trough side of this cycle though, it should be seen as an inevitable part of the movement of their life. Individuals with Double Loops certainly experience the ups and downs of life more intensely than most but are best advised not to fixate on the downward arms of the spiral. The danger here is a disillusionment and disappointment that can lead to depression. Encouragement should be given so they can continue and not give up – a good motto for those with Double Loops is: "Great faith, great doubt… and great determination."

More positively, the Double Loop pattern gives them the ability to see both sides of an issue and thus can give a diplomatic ability that makes them good negotiators or arbitrators. People with Double Loops need to integrate the two sides of the coin they can see, rather than view them as irreconcilable opposites. The Double Loop pattern closely resembles the Taoist yin-yang symbol and it is within Taoism that we find opposites are recognised as being complementary to one another rather than being poles apart. The key therefore is to accept the cyclical nature of life's experience and to recognise that beneath duality there is a fundamental unity. There may indeed be two sides to the coin, but it wouldn't be a coin if it didn't have two sides. The key to resolving the Double Loop dilemma is therefore in reconciling and integrating the opposites in one's experiences, endeavouring to create a balanced appreciation of the different dimensions of human experience. For this reason, those with

Double Loop fingerprints are often drawn to the spiritual side of life.

Fire Dermatoglyphic – Tented Arch

All triradii, wherever they are found in the hand, are ruled by the Fire element. In the Tented Arch, we find the triradius centrally located and pushing a rising spur up towards the tip of the finger. This reveals the fundamentally expressive orientation of the Tented Arch. People with Tented Arches have an abundance of energy and are often intensely enthusiastic. Generally creative and constructive, they have a great need for self-expression and frequently express themselves by taking action. Their enthusiasm means they usually become deeply involved in everything they do, sometimes to the point of zealousness and fanaticism, for their intensity can make them the fanatical devotees of particular causes or "-isms". Hence, they can make good leaders and initiators. They have a highly responsive nature in general, spontaneity comes naturally to them, though they are prone to being somewhat rash or impulsive and can be quite volatile in their behaviour, all things being equal. They are usually effervescent, sociable and outgoing types, but can also be highly sensitive and a bit wired. They like to keep themselves busy – though it is important that they find a useful way of channeling this so they need to find an ideal towards which they can aspire – they need to find a mission in life.

Tented Arch

Air Dermatoglyphics – Whorls and Peacock's Eye

People with Whorls are often highly original and effective individuals. They are independent, freedom loving, self-motivated and often highly talented. Whorls are the most aware of their individuality, often to the point of being too individualistic. They resist being influenced by others and have a strong dislike of interference; they will actively rebel if they are restricted or hampered in any way. Most of all, they have a strong need for personal autonomy. They have a strong desire to be self-sufficient and self-contained, independent of all others. Hence, they tend to be their own person rather than one of the crowd. This contributes to why they can be original – they like to be different!

Frequently, they feel different from other people and this can cause them to be something of a loner. They never lose their sense of individuality, and this sometimes results in an inability to mix with others. Even if they do mix with others, they are still aware of themselves as individuals and find it difficult to adapt to group identities. Most often they will relate to others in an individual, one to one manner, usually choosing to be with other individuals – usually other Whorl types – from any group to which they belong. Otherwise, there can be a great love of solitude. Their solitary nature often results in a feeling of being "out of place" or alienated from others. They often feel that they are misunderstood by others and suffer the feeling that they don't really belong. These are the black sheep of the family, the social outcasts and the misfits. The sooner they get used to the fact that they are never going to fit in, the sooner they will develop the self-acceptance to do their own thing.

The presence of Whorls also indicates a thoughtful and analytical disposition; they are quick thinking and grasp ideas quickly. Their mental alacrity often makes them impatient with other people who they see as plodders. They usually have clearly formed opinions about things and because they brook no interference from others they can be rather argumentative. It's very hard to change their mind or to persuade them to think otherwise. They need to work it out for themselves.

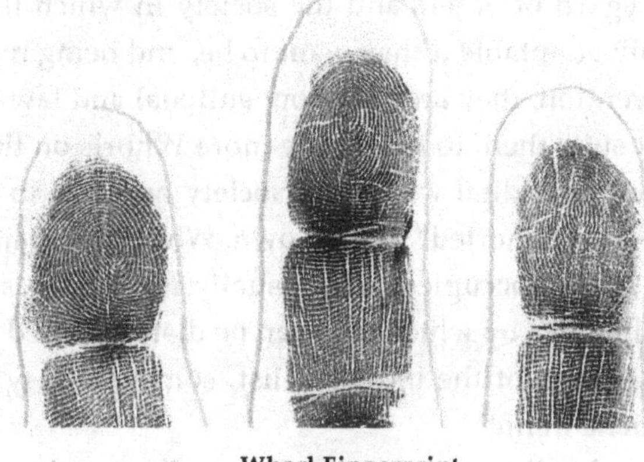

Whorl Fingerprint

Peacock's Eye Fingerprint

Whorls like to be their own boss and hence are drawn to work that involves self-employment or work that gives them a position of control and autonomy. When working for others, they must have their own niche where they have control and can act without reference to others. They need to express their individuality and thus must have the freedom to do so. They rarely express themselves in a subordinate manner, which sometimes can be interpreted as arrogance, and their need for autonomy and control is such that they like to organise things with themselves at the centre.

Many whorled people can be very difficult to get along with. They can be very much a law unto themselves and often have an inward disregard of others and the society in which they live. They are only adaptable if they want to be, and being much less tied by convention, they are only conventional and law-abiding as long as it suits them to be so. The more Whorls on the hand, the more the individual will reject society and live in another dimension – in a "whorled" of their own. Whilst they can appear isolated or self-preoccupied, they usually also possess unique and original talents by which they can be distinguished. For the Whorl is the mark of the individualist, someone busy finding their own niche in life.

The **Peacock's Eye**, or compound, is really a variant pattern from the Whorl and thus carries with it much of the same meaning. The pattern of a Whorl inside a Loop suggests it is somewhat softer than the pure Whorl type but the best way to interpret the Peacock's Eye is as the Whorl – the presence of the kernel of the Whorl is sufficient to make it different from the ordinary Loop pattern. The exception to this is in the very rare case of a Radial Peacock's Eye – which is a Whorl inside a *Radial* Loop! This evident contradiction tends to produce most interesting people, both highly influenced and highly original at the same time! Jimi Hendrix is perhaps the most famous example of someone with a Radial Peacock's Eye fingerprint, as we shall see later.

Other Variant Patterns

Occasionally patterns other than the seven enumerated above are found, but usually these take the form of various combinations of the main pattern types. Only less than one per cent of fingerprint patterns aren't classifiable as any one of the seven types given above. The shape and formation of the pattern itself may reveal something of how the person experiences this in their lives, though the interpretation of these patterns also depends on which of the other pattern types are involved. The meaning of these rare patterns can therefore be derived by combining the qualities of the basic patterns from which they are made up. Any really unusual fingerprint pattern will therefore immediately tell you that there is something really unusual and distinctive about the person!

As you look at the fingerprint, follow the shape of the pattern and describe how it moves. It is useful to consider that the fingerprints are formed as a result of the effects of the impression of consciousness on our psycho-physical being. Describing their shape is to delineate the nature of the paradigmatic vortices of consciousness that seek expression through the very being of the person whose hands you are assessing.

The Assessment of Fingerprint Patterns

The first thing to do when looking at fingerprints is to add up the total number of each type of fingerprint. If you have three or more Arches, you have an Arch dominant hand. If you have five or more Whorls, you have a Whorl dominant hand. In the case of Loops, it needs to be seven or more Loops. A hand with five Loops and five Whorls will be someone who oscillates between wanting to be part of a group and wanting to spend time on their own.

With regard to the minor fingerprint patterns, the presence of just one of them is sufficient for that pattern to have a big effect in that person's life. In the case of the Double Loop, that's when it is found on the Thumb. Two Double Loops is a lot, especially if one is also found on the Index finger. In the case of both Radial Loops and Tented Arches, given that these patterns are so rare, finding even one in a hand will have a big impact in their consciousness, not least because when found, it is usually seen on the Index finger.

So, the second thing to assess is the fingerprint on the Index finger. The Index finger is a significant indicator of someone's sense of self and their sense of personal identity so the fingerprint here says a great deal about who they are, how they see themselves and how they feel about themselves. It is the keystone fingerprint. If you were only going to analyse one thing from a hand, look at this pattern. It is the most differentiated dermatoglyphic feature.

When analysing the fingerprints, follow this approach. Identify:

- the overall fingerprint type,
- the fingerprint on the Index finger,
- the odd fingerprint out,
- the anomalous fingerprint, and
- compare homologous fingerprints.

Only then consider the significance of each fingerprint on each of the fingers.

Once you have found out what the dominant fingerprint pattern type is and which pattern is on their Index finger, then look for the odd one out. The fingerprint that is different from all the others on their hands will often represent something that is very important to them, their point of difference, what makes them feel unique and different. In a hand of eight Loops, the place where the Whorl is found will be an area of life that is very important to them. The singular Arch in a hand will assume a greater importance and significance in that person's life because of its singularity.

Fourthly, look for any *anomalous* or misplaced fingerprint. What I mean by that is look for the fingerprint that shouldn't be there! This is the fingerprint that is unusual by virtue of statistical distribution. For example, an Arch on the Ring finger is rare when it is found at all – but it is extremely rare if there are not already 5–6 other Arch prints in the hands! Similarly, a Whorl on the Little finger is really very unusual if found by itself, as a Whorl only usually occurs on the Little finger when whorls are already found on all other eight digits. If you find an anomalous fingerprint, that print usually takes on a greater significance in that person's life.

Next, look at the *homologous* fingerprints – that is to say, compare the fingerprints on the same fingers on the left and right hands and look to see whether the fingerprints are different or the same. Where the same finger has the same fingerprint, the qualities associated with that finger and fingerprint are strengthened and become more important in their life. Differences in the fingerprints from one hand to the other will show a growth, a change, a development of the person as they "move" from the Passive hand fingerprint to the Active hand fingerprint. How they feel and understand a finger internally is different from how they outwardly express it in the world. This will describe something of the fundamental conflicts and struggles they experience in trying to reconcile the effects of each of these different dermatoglyphic types.

Finally, consider the significance of each fingerprint as it is found on each of the fingers.

Fingerprint Interpretation

A quick note about how to approach interpreting your fingerprint patterns: it's important to remember that humans are complex and contradictory beings! Working out the overall fingerprint pattern type is a good way of getting a general feel of a person, whether they are a more sociable and group-oriented person or more of a loner; or whether family is very important to them, for example. But analysing the details of the finger and palmar patterns will reveal more specifically what a person is like and what motivates them – and the impulses shown by these patterns may or may not always sit comfortably together.

The dermatoglyphic patterns show what we are disposed towards, what motivates us and what drives us. By correctly identifying the most important fingerprint and palmar patterns, we will be able to see the primary motivational forces within a person that will inform the choices that they make *throughout their whole life.* It is therefore important to get our analysis right. Take your time.

Fingers and Fingerprints

As we have seen, the first thing to do when analysing the fingerprints is to add up the total numbers of fingerprints to see which is the dominant fingerprint pattern type. This will indicate the predominant psychological orientation of the person overall, which will correspond with the outlines for each of the fingerprint pattern types previously given. However, it is not always the case that you will count six or more of one type of fingerprint, so making this assessment is not always clear cut. In practice, having five Whorls will indicate someone who is Whorl dominant; and having only three Arches will be enough for the characteristics of the Arch pattern to come through as very important. Some fingerprint patterns can have a dominant effect even if they are not numerically dominant. Whilst this is true for a hand with just two Double Loops or one Tented Arch, it is especially true of the Radial Loop pattern.

The significant factor to consider is where the fingerprint pattern type is to be found. Clearly, the significance of each of the fingerprint pattern types differs as they are found on each of the different digits. Although we have outlined the general significance of the fingerprint patterns themselves, they are interpreted slightly differently, depending on the fingers on which they occur.

Index Finger and the Thumb

The fingerprint pattern on the Index finger can be considered the keynote pattern of the hand. If you only have time to read one thing from a hand, then it is the dermatoglyphic on the Index finger that you need to look at. Whatever pattern is found here will be very descriptive of the person's individuality, not least because the Index finger exhibits the greatest variety of dermatoglyphic patterns of all the fingers. Due to the fact that Ulnar Loops are much less common here than on other fingers, all of the other fingerprint patterns can occur more frequently, including all the minor patterns. The dermatoglyphic here is also important because of the significance of the Index finger itself. Of all the digits, this finger is the most significant descriptor of our sense of self and self-identity. The fingerprint pattern found here therefore reveals something of our personal sense of who we are. It shows the dermatoglyphic patterning we most closely identify with.

The fingerprint pattern on the Thumb is also important to consider in its own right, for the Thumb is all about how we direct our lives and how we express ourselves in the world. The dermatoglyphic pattern here will indicate how we come across to others, how we are experienced by them. Therefore, it is always important to compare the fingerprint patterns of the Thumb and the Index finger together as this will give considerable clues into any conflicts the individual experiences between their own and other's views of themselves or between what they want for themselves and how they go about getting it.

Fingerprint Combinations

There are some interesting combinations that are commonly found in Caucasian hands. For example, eight Ulnar Loops with two Whorls on both the Ring fingers shows someone who is essentially conformist but who seeks to express their individuality through their appearance, fashion and their own personal style. Someone with predominantly Ulnar Loops in their hands but with Whorls on their Index fingers is a team player who works well with others – but they want to be the Team Captain! In general, the Whorl-Ulnar Loop balance is a very important one to check, as this describes the balance they negotiate between doing things with others and doing things on their own, depending on exactly where the fingerprints are. A hand with five Whorls and five Ulnar Loops will always be trying to balance those two demands.

As we have already seen, the different pattern types occur in different frequencies on each of the fingers. It is important to familiarize ourselves with these distributions to at least some extent, because only by so doing will we be able to correctly determine the importance of a particular fingerprint to the individual concerned – whether that is because it denotes a particular psychological orientation or indicates a specific skill or attribute. For example, it is not expected to see a Whorl on the Little finger unless all the other fingers have Whorls. Equally, it is unexpected to see an Arch on the Earth finger if there is not an Arch on the Index finger as well. In general, the rarer the occurrence of the pattern, the greater the importance it assumes or reveals in the consciousness of the individual, particularly if it is an anomalous or unexpected pattern.

It needs to be noted that there are some fingerprints that are so rarely found that it is not yet clear what they might signify on specific fingers. This is especially true of Tented Arches and Radial Loops but also somewhat true of Double Loop fingerprints. For the purposes of interpretation, Peacock's Eyes/Compounds are considered as Whorls and are not treated separately here.

Dermatoglyphic Patterns on the Water (Index) Finger – Personal Identity

The dermatoglyphic pattern on the Index finger reveals much of the individual's sense of self-identity. As a corollary of this, it reflects something of their self-confidence and self-esteem as well as indicating something of their personal values and spiritual beliefs. It is the core pattern of identity.

Ulnar Loop (30–35%)

The Ulnar Loop, a water element print on the Water finger, shows someone who identifies closely with how they feel. They have an easy-going personality and are flexible; they mix well with others and are sociable. Their sense of who they are is highly influenced by the mood they are in and so, like water, their sense of confidence and self-worth ebbs and flows, rising and falling with the tides of their emotions.

One of the things that is most important to them is acceptance, being accepting of others and being accepted by others. There is a strong identification with their social group or community and they feel good about themselves when they have a sense of belonging. They are naturally group-oriented and want to feel included. They work best in, and feel most suited to, cooperative teamwork. They don't like it when people are argumentative or critical; being tolerant and sensitive to other people's feelings is important to them.

More of a follower than a leader, they prefer a democratic organisation where everyone gets to have their say and where everyone's views are held equally valid. They value being part of something but can get caught up in fads and groupthink; they can be far too tolerant of things that are not good for them or the community in which they find themselves. Often their need for the emotional security of belonging can override their critical thinking ability, and they can lose the sense of their own personal identity in a group. They are good at adapting to changing circumstances and being accommodating and hence have versatility, but because of their need to fit in with others, they can lack independence.

Since they feel good about themselves when they have established their friend group or have found their tribe, they hate it when people are divisive or argumentative. They want acceptance and inclusivity. In their spirituality, they value forgiveness, tolerance and compassion.

Whorl (21–25%)

A Whorl on the Index finger shows someone with a strong sense of their own individuality and a very strong need for autonomy, freedom and independence. People with a Whorl on this finger feel good about themselves when they have the freedom to do things the way that they want to do them. They like being in charge and like to be their own boss. They particularly don't like being told what to do by others so, if you give them a task to do, leave them to it. Someone with a Whorl on the Water finger needs to be working for themselves or be in charge of the task they are assigned to or have a high degree of autonomy in the role that they have in the organisation. Natural leaders, they like to organise things with themselves at the centre. Their leadership style is more autocratic than democratic, as they generally know best! They see themselves as self-contained and self-reliant and want to encourage others to be self-reliant too. There is a disdain of sycophants and people who lack independence in thought and opinion. They can't stand going with the crowd and have the view that if everyone is going off in one direction then the best thing is to go in the opposite direction. Theirs is a philosophy of independence and self-reliance.

Generally non-conformist and with the ability to form their own opinions, they are strongly attracted to unusual philosophies and belief-systems and so tend to have idiosyncratic values. These are the pioneers and reformists, the people who come up with new ideas and new ways of doing things. They like to have space and freedom in their life and their self-esteem is generally augmented when they are doing something individual – they feel good with themselves when they are doing something original or unconventional. Their life lesson is to learn to come to terms with being different; the sooner they have a deep acceptance of this, the sooner they can live a life that is an expression of their quirky individuality.

Radial Loop (18–24%)

The Radial Loop on the Index finger shows someone whose sense of self-identity is very strongly affected by the people and circumstances around them. Because the Radial Loop opens from the Thumb side of the hand, they are very much more influenced by the opinions and expectations of others and often try and fit in with what they think others want them to be. This can be very problematic for them if they are around strong or domineering people. Often their relationship with their parents is or was difficult, especially if their parents had high expectations of them. Women with this pattern often experience their mother as having been critical or judgemental.

With a childhood of "not being good enough" those with Radial Loops on their Water fingers often end up with a lack of self-belief, low self-confidence and low self-esteem. They are very sensitive to other people's expectations and hence are very sensitive to critique from others. To avoid any further criticism, they tend to adapt who and what they are to fit in with the world around them. People with Radial Loops on the finger of identity work very hard to do everything "right" because they really want to avoid being "wrong" – because if they get something wrong, they will be criticised and told off, and they really want to not have that experience again. As a result, in personal relationships, they can become people-pleasers or can lose themselves in the identity of another person. In their work life, they make very good employees, working extra hard to not meet with any disapprobation or disapproval.

Those with Radial Loops here feel good about themselves when they receive positive feedback; their confidence is augmented when they receive encouragement. If you encounter a child with this fingerprint pattern on their Index finger, have a word with their parents and let them know how sensitive their child is and remind them to constantly encourage and support their child and avoid criticising them for not being "good enough". These individuals need approbation not disapprobation, carrot not stick.

It's as if those with Radial Loops are born with no armour or protection and are unable to deflect critical comments, no matter how subtly expressed. Criticism goes right through them and pierces them straight in the heart. They take all commentary very personally and it affects them deeply. Essentially, those with Radial Loops are highly sensitised to the world around them. They take on board other people's feelings and moods, so they are strongly affected by the vibe of the space that they are in. Often, they are not sure if what they are feeling is their own feeling or a feeling that they have picked up from those around them.

In the hands of women, this pattern gives a very strongly empathic disposition and it is notable that Radial Loops are found often on the Water fingers of carers, counsellors and therapists or where being sympathetically responsive to the personalised needs of the customer is very important, such as hairdressers and beauticians. Anyone with a Radial Loop on this finger is good at listening and paying attention to the needs of others, once they can get over their own fear of being judged. Their leadership style is to listen and to give feedback. Their personal philosophy of life emphasises the importance of self-acceptance.

In some cases, having a Radial Loop here makes the person hypervigilant, always scanning the room to see how they need to be. They are always anticipating other people's needs, always watching and looking out "how to behave" and "what's the right thing to be doing". Especially in the hands of men, a Radial Loop on the Index finger can make them very defensive. They sense that they have a vulnerability and feel very uncomfortable about it, which often makes them very defensive, especially to criticism. Men with Radial Loops here can act in quite contrarian or rebellious ways as a deliberate reaction so as *not* to be influenced and it is a curious fact that Radial Loops are found more frequently in the hands of men who practise karate and other forms of self-defence than you would normally expect to see.

For these reasons it is vitally important that those with Radial Loops choose their close friends carefully. They need to stay away from people who put them down or who are critical or sarcastic, as they have no defence against that, especially if they have internalised a childhood experience of critical parenting. Secondly, they need to choose their social groups very carefully – because they will become like whatever situation or circumstance they find themselves in. Those with Radial Loop fingerprints mould themselves to others and osmotically adopt the attitudes and values of those who are around them. This pattern is very chameleonic, which is to say that, like a chameleon, they change their colour, shape and appearance according to the environment they are in. Their sense of who they are changes according to whom they are with. They therefore tend to have unrealistic perceptions of themselves, either because they've adopted the identity of the people they're with as their own or, because their sense of themselves is based on how others see them, rather than from within themselves. Because they borrow so much from others, they often have blind spots about themselves. They think they are what they draw in.

The upside of this "superpower" is an ability to adapt themselves to meet other people, to fit in with other people, to accommodate to the needs and world views of others. The downside of this pattern is losing themselves in the values, opinions and expectations of others. As their self-identity changes so much and they identify with the people, persons, situation or environment they find themselves within, it's very hard for them to have a clear idea of who they are. They can easily lose themselves in the ideas, aims, requirements or personalities of others. In situations where they are around dominant and forceful characters, it is quite possible for them to completely lose their own identity in the other, for example, a wife with a dominant husband may lose all sight of her own individual path in life through her adoption of a common identity with her spouse.

Very often, those people with Radial Loops effect extreme changes in their lives because, in order to become themselves again, they have to make a complete break with those they have previously been involved with. Change of friendship circles, break up of a marriage or long-term relationship, change of job, anything where the environment around them has dominated them so much they lost sight of themselves, has to be radically altered in order for them to find themselves again.

Fundamentally, what is needed for those with Radial Loops on their Water fingers is to spend time on their own. When they have time and space by themselves, outside the company of all others, they can see who they are and what they want in life quite apart from other people's expectations of them. They therefore need to create space in their lives where they can be alone with themselves, without any input from anyone or anything else.

Of course, because their whole sense of who they are is so interwoven with their interrelation with others it can be very difficult for them to break free of those influences. But when those with Radial Loops can find time to be by themselves, remove themselves from situations in which their fear of being judged by others occurs, they can be liberated from the habit of thinking they must live up to other people's expectations. Mindfulness meditation practices, embodiment practices or mindful yoga practices will greatly assist with this.

Once the person has become aware of the effects of being so open to others, life becomes much easier for those with Radial Loops. They can mindfully watch and see their reactivity and then *choose* how they want to respond to the situations around them. But time and space on their own is essential for them to get that perspective. Learning to see that their self-worth and who they are is not dependent on the opinions and expectations of others is a crucial step in their self-development. They need to develop a more realistic perception of themselves based on their individual talents and abilities and be less dependent on others for their self-esteem and sense of identity.

Arch (7–14%)

Arches are an Earth element print. Someone with an Arch on their Index finger sees themselves as a practical and down-to-earth person who likes to be useful and to help other people. They are the support person, the carer, the nurturer, the provider. They feel good about themselves when they can give practical assistance to others. Family and family life is important to them. Loyal and respectful, they seek security and stability in their own lives and in the lives of those around them. They dislike dishonesty and if you break their trust, it's hard to win it back. Betrayal is a deal-breaker for them. Arches on the Water finger of women are often seen in the hands of teachers, nurses, social workers and in caring roles where providing and supporting others are key functions. The Arch is good at "holding space" in which those they support can be nurtured and cared for. Generally, they develop good practical abilities through the acquisition of some form of skill, as they find it easiest to express who and what they are through doing something *useful*.

In men, the Arch on this finger draws them to learn skills and trades, so is commonly seen in the hands of technicians, electricians, carpenters and handymen. The acquisition of any practical skill is always a good idea as far as they are concerned, because this means they can then readily get a job, which means they can earn money – which in turn means they can create stability and security in their life. Financial security is important to them, not for materialistic or acquisitive reasons, but because once they have financial security, they can then purchase the house or whatever they need to create a sense of security. From there, they then have the stable environment in which they can have a family.

People with Arches on their Water finger have an innate sense of caution and reserve that can inhibit their spontaneity. Sometimes, this self-containment is due to a sense of duty or responsibility to others, and so they may repress their own needs and requirements in order to be of aid or assistance to others. This is due, at least in part, to the fact that they have a strong sense of justice and fairness. This may be enough to create the inclination to do some form of legal work or work that is aimed to rebalance injustices in our society. They make trustworthy and reliable employees. In terms of their personal philosophy, they are often attracted to belief systems which demonstrate a respect for, or an affinity with, nature i.e. the Earth. Otherwise, they may seek allegiance with the more traditional or conventional belief systems of the culture in which they are born.

Double Loop (1–7%)

The Double Loop on the Index finger indicates someone who has an unclear picture of themselves and who may find the whole concept of "self-identity" a bit of a mystery. Because they feel everything so deeply, their sense of who they are is very fluid and changeable. As the two sides to the Double Loop show, they get emotionally pulled in two directions – they feel the highs and they feel the lows. Life for them is an emotional rollercoaster and can bring them much in the way of confusion and uncertainty, particularly about how they feel about something.

They often experience a lot of doubt, especially about relationships and how they are feeling in relationships. Anyone who is a partner of someone with a Double Loop on their Index finger must expect to go on this roller-coaster journey of emotions with them. They experience their emotions very intensely and this can be very destabilising. Doubt and self-questioning can undermine their self-confidence, their belief in themselves and their belief in any relationship that they are in.

This fluctuating sense of self creates duality in other aspects of their lives. They generally experience a conflict with regards to their personal ideals and ambitions, vacillating between alternatives and can be unclear about what they want for themselves. Their lives can become a muddle as they find it difficult to make clear and distinct choices about what they want to do. They find it difficult to make decisions sometimes to the extent that they feel stuck, like they are caught in a rip current at sea and can't move forward or backwards. They need time to weigh things up to evaluate the best way to proceed. A favourite answer to any question is "I don't know" or "I'm not sure" sometimes simply because they can't see things sufficiently clearly to choose between them but also because, sometimes, they are just not keen to be fixed into any position due to being able to see both sides of the situation.

Positively applied, they can use this ability to good effect. They often make good negotiators, diplomats or mediators as they can present a balanced perspective, precisely because they consider both sides of any issue. Theirs is a philosophy that seeks to reconcile conflicts and to create more peace and harmony in the world. They are very accepting of all beliefs and religions. Those with Double Loops on their Water finger often have a more spiritual take on the world because of this. The dermatoglyphic itself looks like the *yin-yang*, the ancient Chinese symbol of integration and the reconciliation of opposites. This is always a useful thing to explain to those with this fingerprint pattern because in the Western view, opposites are so often viewed as antagonistic to each other – good versus bad, day versus night, up versus down etc. But in the Chinese symbolism, the *yin-yang* shows us that actually opposites are *complementary* – you can't have up without down, day without night etc. The solution to the conflict that those with Double Loops feel is to find a way in which to avoid thinking in terms of *either-or* and instead find solutions that are *both-and,* finding a synthesis to integrate the options in the dilemma.

Tented Arch (2–6%)

Tented Arches are rarely found on the Index finger but when seen show someone who has an outgoing and sociable temperament with a great deal of enthusiasm. They like to take the initiative and are usually not afraid of being in the limelight, so they generally evince good leadership potential. Sometimes their enthusiasm can border on single-mindedness or even obsession. They tend to espouse "causes" or ideals and apply themselves intensely to the task at hand. What is most important for those with a Tented Arch on the Water finger is to have a "mission", somewhere to direct their energy and enthusiasm. One good example I know is a vegan activist who organises meetings, events and political actions to fervently try and convert the world to a vegan diet. Another is a man who held a vision for a whole new, better style of festival, which a few years later he actually brought to fruition. One of the women who pioneered the nearly viral phenomenon of "Light Language" has a Tented Arch here, as does a leading figure in the Human Design movement who brought it to spread throughout New Zealand. I have even met a 10-year-old with a Tented Arch who was so focussed on saving the whales, he got his whole class at school to do a entire term's project on the subject! These are people busy putting the world "to right" according to the vision of their ideals. Having a focus point for their enthusiasm and energy is essential for them to find meaning in their life.

Dermatoglyphic Patterns on the Earth (Middle) Finger – Cultural Identity

The dermatoglyphic pattern on the Earth finger reveals something of the person's relationship to authority and conventions, their attitude to rules and structures, their views both political and philosophical, plus their relationship to the culture they are born into and the cultural values that they hold. It reveals something of the attitudes they have with regard to society and its traditions and conventions. Equally, it can reflect their attitudes to home and family life, to possessions and wealth and to career and their role in society.

Ulnar Loop (66–74%)

The Ulnar Loop on the Earth finger shows that the person generally holds conventional beliefs and values, going along with and accepting the general consensus of their society and its rules and regulations. They value people working together as a group (the loop) and so endeavour to fit into society and are therefore generally law abiding. The Ulnar Loop here gives an open-mindedness which does not bind them to any one particular political, moral or religious doctrine. Their values are rather more flexible and accommodating (water) and they value tolerance and the acceptance of others' views and beliefs. There can be a political preference for democracy and a strong appreciation of social cohesion and social order. There is an innate appreciation of material things for the ease or pleasure they bring and hence a desire to provide a comfortable home for their family and themselves.

Whorl (13–15%)

A Whorl on the Earth finger shows that they are decidedly unconventional! These are people who like to think for themselves and so tend to be argumentative. They don't like to be told what to believe or want to think and would rather work it out for themselves. There is a strong dislike of authority figures and people in power – and a level of disdain for people who are very conventional. For these are not people who uphold conventional norms and mores – and as we have seen in the Scotland Yard statistics, Whorls on the Earth finger can be seen slightly more frequently in the hands of criminals than the general population. Not that that means that they have criminal tendencies; rather they have a uniquely developed sense of law and order and tend to hold self-determined philosophical and moral values. They are conventional only in so far as it suits them to be so, and otherwise may completely disregard prevailing customs and traditions to the point even of flouting the law. Consequently, they are attracted to more unusual values and beliefs and may well belong to unusual sects, groups, gangs or cults.

There is a strong belief in the individual and this may well be reflected in their political beliefs. There is generally something unusual about their home or their domestic environment in some way and they may either be disinterested in material possessions or be attracted to collect strange or unusual things. In any case, their home and possessions will be a manifestation of their individuality. They will seek to express their individuality in their working life too, and so will be attracted to an unusual or unconventional career. Generally, there is a dislike of being tied down and so, responsibilities are usually accepted only if they are self-created. An anomalous Whorl on this finger can show an ability to conduct original research, being a science lab researcher or even perhaps possessing a talent for musical composition. Whorls on both Earth fingers shows an innovator and researcher, a pioneer of new ways of doing things.

Arch (5–13%)

The Arch on the Earth finger shows they have a strong sense of order and so are drawn to clear-cut and uncomplicated systems of belief. They are naturally suspicious of anything too complex or metaphysical and prefer instead practical and useful systems of belief or codes which have stood the test of time. This can make them quite traditional in their values or can indicate an interest in demonstrable belief systems such as science. Their strong sense of order and a quest for certainty may manifest as a desire to uncover the rules that structure material things and hence an interest in scientific research such as biology or physics. Equally there can be an interest in ecology and environmental justice.

In more elevated individuals, there may be an affiliation with spiritual systems with an emphasis on nature or natural energies or cycles such as paganism, moon cycles and seasonal celebrations. There is also usually a fundamentally strong sense of justice and fairness, particularly with regard to the application of laws in society and there may be a corresponding impulse to assist those who suffer injustice. Interested in criminology and anthropology, this pattern can be seen in the hands of social workers, those who want to work with the less fortunate, accountants and those in the law profession. The Arch here gives a strong sense of duty and responsibility and an urge to provide security for their family and themselves and hence they desire a stable career that can produce this security. Often, they will seek work that makes use of their developed sense of justice.

Double Loop (2–4%)

The Double Loop on the Earth finger can show there is a strong sense of conflict of cultural values, such as may be produced by being born into a traditional Moslem or Hindu family but growing up in secular British culture. Here, they are strongly affected by two conflicting cultural traditions and though they can see the value of both, they may feel torn as to which set of values they should follow. Alternatively, they may be able to integrate these two but not usually without experiencing some degree of conflict and confusion. This confusion may of course originate from their experience of their family and may produce a profound lack of clear cultural identity, which can be psychologically destabilising. More simply, they may just experience a certain ambiguity regarding their own moral, ethical or political standpoint, which is something that they need to seek to resolve in this lifetime.

In New Zealand, when this pattern occurs in the hands of Maori people, there is a very strong awareness of a bi-cultural heritage and often a deliberate intention to try and reconcile these two. For those who have been brought up with *Pakeha* (white man's) values, there is often strong interest in learning *Te Reo Maori* (Maori language) and re-familiarising themselves with *tikanga Maori* (Maori values) and bringing these two sides of New Zealand's culture together. Political and cultural integration is paramount when there is a Double Loop on the middle finger.

Otherwise, this double loop can create a sense of confusion in a person's philosophical beliefs. In particular, they can feel a strong conflict between material and spiritual values which often produces a lot of soul searching. It may also produce confusion with regard to career choices and may provoke an endless searching for the "right" job. There may be some confusion or instability in their financial or domestic affairs or a persistent sense of guilt over material possessions.

Radial Loop (2–3%)

A Radial Loop on the Earth finger is rare and its significance is difficult to determine, not least because it's hard for people to articulate their understanding of how they come to align with cultural norms. However, the nature of this pattern suggests that they might find it easy to adapt to and take on board the customs of other cultures. Ask them if they enjoy travelling or like to spend a portion of the year in a foreign country and if they feel they easily assimilate other cultural norms. Let me know what you discover.

Tented Arch (1–2%)

These people are often the enthusiastic followers of "-isms" with an inclination to get involved with radical religious or political ideologies. Their intensity and enthusiasm are directed towards creating changes in the world of politics and society. In other words, they want to "change the system" and consequently may espouse revolutionary politics – or, if they are more conservative, they may be more attracted to fundamentalist religious movements. Either way, they are inclined towards radical politics, whether that is of a revolutionary or a reactionary nature, depending on other hand features.

Dermatoglyphic Patterns on the Fire (Ring) Finger – Social Identity

The dermatoglyphic pattern on the Fire finger reveals something of how the individual expresses themselves, both in terms of their appearance and their social interaction with others and in terms of artistic creativity.

Ulnar Loop (51–62%)

The Ulnar Loop on the Fire finger gives a strong interest in art, especially sensitivity to colour, but gives more of an *appreciation* of things artistic rather than an original artistic talent. Their personal tastes in clothes and fashion tend to be less expressive of their individuality and there can be a tendency to follow fashions rather than initiate them. They generally like socialising with others and so are fond of group activities. They easily and readily adapt to other people and have a strong need to feel that they belong. Good at working in teams or groups.

Whorl (28–38%)

A Whorl on this finger shows some unique or original form of self-expression. This may take the form of an unusual dress sense, with unusual tastes in clothes, fashion, style or colour combinations. They have idiosyncratic aesthetic tastes and so generally tend not to follow fashions. The Whorl here gives an unusual sense of design and harmony and so they may even work in the fields of design, fashion, beauty etc. Even if they do not work in these fields, their personal forms of self-expression will be characterised by their individual tastes. Their appearance may be unusual in some manner or else they might utilise their original sense of colour and design in the way they decorate their home. In any case, they like to express their individuality and are not bound by conventional aesthetic mores. They tend to be more independent in a crowd and in social situations and often have some unusual hobbies or pastimes. The Whorl on the Ring finger can be a strong indicator of artistic talent or design ability, particularly if the Ring finger is itself long and it is the only digit to bear a Whorl, as can be seen in the hands of artists, actors and musicians.

Arch (2–4%)

An Arch on the Fire finger shows someone who can find it difficult to express themselves in a group or in social situations – too much Earth puts out Fire. They can prefer to stay at home rather than go out socialising as they feel reserved, which can make it difficult for them to relax or open up socially. They would rather stay in and have a family meal than go out partying. Arches on the Ring finger can show practical art interests and skills. They like to practically express their creativity making things such as clothing, designing jewellery or hat making etc. In particular they are attracted to traditional crafts and skills, or art forms that utilise more earthy materials such as clay or stone and are likely to be naturally gifted in arts such as sculpture, woodwork, carving, weaving or even traditional tattooing. Aesthetically, they like the beauty of natural materials and they may decorate their home with these even if they are not artisans. They may also be drawn to the simple beauty of indigenous crafts and artefacts.

Double Loop (1-2%)

The Double Loop when found on the Ring finger can show someone who experiences anxiety in social situations and yet is perceived by others as being someone who is confident and self-assured. Their internal experience is one of self-doubt in social environments – how are they being perceived? How are they coming across to others? "Am I good enough in this social situation?" An internal feeling of uncertainty about how to present themselves and interact with others causes an oscillation in their social experience from being fully sociable one moment to becoming fully withdrawn the next. Artistically, these are the type of people who keep changing their mind about what they want to create and so end up with a cupboard full of unfinished art projects.

Radial Loop (1%)

The Radial Loop on the Ring finger is found on people who are exceptionally sociable. They are very responsive to other people so social interaction is of considerable importance to them. Their reputation may be very important to them. This person will fit in easily with groups and adopt the surroundings as their own, feeling at home nearly everywhere. This Loop indicates an attitude of shared pleasures with others, i.e. they get pleasure from other people's enjoyment. They are keen to make sure everyone is happy and that everyone is enjoying themselves; they may make the perfect host or entertainer. In a way, their own sense of happiness is dependent on the happiness of those around them and so they don't feel they can have a good time unless everyone else is too. They can make very good mimics or impersonators as they are good at "role playing" being someone else, for example, they would be more likely to enjoy karaoke or being in a covers band than playing originals. Because they may be a very good mimic or copyist, this could even manifest as them being a forger! It should be noted that Radial Loop fingerprints on the Fire finger are much more common in the hands of those with Down Syndrome – which perhaps goes some way to explain their highly sociable nature. People with Down Syndrome are very friendly and responsive to others and clearly derive great pleasure from other people's enjoyment.

Dermatoglyphic Patterns on the Air (Little) Finger – Communicative Identity

The dermatoglyphic pattern on the Air finger shows something of a person's style of interpersonal communication and thus may reflect how they actually speak and think, as well as reflecting something of their attitudes to sex, sexuality and relationships.

Ulnar Loop (80–87%)

The Ulnar Loop is so overwhelmingly predominant on the Air finger that it only serves to signify relative normality in terms of the values someone holds with respect to relationships. Most people want connection and closeness in intimate relationships and want to have a sense of being together, of merging with another. That is the Water element on the Air finger – importance is attached to the emotional quality of relationships and to making intimate connections through emotional self-expression with another. They are generally conventional in their approaches to relationships and in their sexual attitudes but check their Water line and Upper Minor line variations. At an intellectual level, an Ulnar Loop here shows they are adaptable and responsive to new ideas and have some degree of versatility in verbal self-expression. Communication is seen as an important means of connecting with other people. If it is the sole Ulnar Loop on the fingers, there may be a heightened sensitivity to the subtleties of the spoken word and an affinity with emotionally laden vocabulary such as poetry or literature or symbolism.

Whorl (9–12%)

A Whorl on the Air finger shows someone who has a highly inventive mind and has unusual ways of expressing themselves. They may use language in novel or idiosyncratic fashions and often are able to present ideas in a strikingly original way. Hence, they make good orators or public speakers, for they have good powers of verbal self-expression and an original talent for communicating their ideas. They are interested in studying the unusual and so are capable of conducting highly original research. Learning languages and an interest in music or musical theory may also be evident in those with this Whorl. They are often unusually eloquent and articulate, not least because it is very unusual to have a Whorl here unless there are Whorls on all the other fingers. However, if it is an anomalous Whorl, this can be indicative of communicative difficulties. If it is the only Whorl on the fingers, there can be a sense of isolation from others and hence difficulties in personal relationships. Here, there can be a feeling of being misunderstood and sometimes problems in clearly communicating their ideas to others.

In terms of relationships, those with a Whorl on the little finger have a great need for space and freedom, meaning that their relationships tend to be somewhat unconventional, if not unusual. They may aspire to having "open" relationships, or they may hold unorthodox attitudes about sexuality and sex, especially if other features of the hands support this. More commonly, their need for freedom and space in their relationships means that they will endeavour to create structures in their relationship to give them that freedom and space. For example, very often they are happiest in long-distance relationships, where they live in a different city from their partner. That way they get to see each other on weekends but have the five days in between to themselves! In extreme cases I have encountered, this need for space can even manifest as having a relationship with someone who is living in a different country. As another example, one couple I know did shift work that was out of sync with each other, so they passed each other in the corridor; as one was getting up to go to work, the other was going to bed! In long-term relationships or with a married couple, there is a need to create their own space in their living arrangement, such as having their own study, art room or studio, where they can get the peace, quiet and solitude they need. It makes perfect sense to such couples that they have separate bedrooms.

Arch (1–3%)

It is rare to find an Arch on the Air finger unless it is part of a set. An Arch here suggests they may have difficulties expressing themselves and difficulties in communicating with others. They are often better at writing things down than at verbally expressing themselves. One highly illustrative example was of a woman who prepared Braille books, Braille being the language of communication through touch! On a more academic-type hand, the Arch here might suggest a careful and cautious researcher, someone who likes to delve deep and get to the bottom of things. Otherwise, it reveals someone who likes to use their mind in a practical way, someone who would rather get on and do something rather than talk. Sexually, the Arch here is indicative of a degree of reticence and inhibition. There may be blocks around their sexual expressiveness or they may feel their communication is somehow thwarted in personal relationships.

Double Loop (1–2%)

The Double Loop is rarely seen on the Air finger but has distinctive consequences if it is found, namely that the person with this pattern experiences some confusion or lack of clarity about their emotional and sexual expression. They could be unclear about what they want from a relationship or uncertain and hesitant in initiating relationships. They experience a greater intensity of confusion and uncertainly in this area of life than is usual, especially when under the age of 22 years. This could manifest in bisexuality, di-morphism, non-binary gender identification or any other permutation of variant sex/gender expression. Double Loops always feel things deeply and with this pattern on this finger, there may be quite wild swings from one form of sex/gender expression to another. An appropriate contemporary term might be "gender fluid". Learning to curb their doubts and developing willingness to embrace all sides of themselves will be very useful in diminishing the ambiguities they experience in their relationships with others.

At an intellectual and communicative level, the Double Loop here gives rise to confusions and uncertainties in the realm of ideas. They may be unclear about what they think about things, and they may have difficulties expressing what they think with clarity. Intellectually, they are always able to see both sides of any issue, which if positively handled shows an ability to reconcile opposing points of view and could point to a diplomatic or tactful nature.

Tented Arches and *Radial Loops*

These patterns are almost never seen on the Air finger so any suggestion of what they might signify can only be suggestive rather than indicative. In one recent example of a Radial Loop on an Air finger, a woman said that she shaped her communication to fit the person she was talking to, changing the sound of her voice and what she said to suit the person she was speaking to. So, this pattern may show a capacity to communicate effectively with others, a useful skill in a medical setting or in counselling and therapeutic work; but more research needs to be done to be sure.

Dermatoglyphic Patterns on the Thumb

The dermatoglyphic pattern on the Thumb reveals the inherent pattern of self-motivation of the individual. It reveals how the person sets about doing things in life, how they enact their wishes and desires in the external world. Fundamentally, it reveals the manner in which they express their will and the manner in which they exert their willpower in the world around them. It shows how they come across to others.

Ulnar Loop (60–64%)

The Ulnar Loop on the Thumb shows someone who is really only motivated to do something if they feel like it. They have to "get in the mood" or cultivate the right feeling-state before they are motivated to do something. Their determination to succeed depends on how they feel or on the strength of feeling they have for the endeavour at hand. They usually find it easier to do things with the help of other people around them, finding the support of other people motivation in and of itself.

They are generally laid back and easy-going, adaptable and accommodating to new or changing circumstances and are not too pushy. The Ulnar Loop person understands the virtues of working together with others. They often like having music in the background as this can lift their mood and "push" them along. They like assistance and the sense of camaraderie that comes from doing things together with other people. Being aware of the needs of others, they are considerate of the aims and intentions of others. This makes them cooperative but can mean they accommodate to the concerns of others, sometimes to the point of self-compromise.

Whorl (18–25%)

In contrast, the Whorl on the Thumb indicates someone who will only flourish if they can do their own thing on their own terms and in their own way. This is the dermatoglyphic indicator *par excellence* for self-employment. They require autonomy and will tolerate no interference from others. They will rebel if others try to impose their will upon them and this can manifest as an unwillingness to compromise. These people are highly self-motivated and their strong self-conviction can give them a certain stubbornness and fixity of will. They are motivated to do things that give them freedom, independence and autonomy. They prefer to do things on their own rather than in a group. They don't like consultation with others as they believe others will either hold them back, not understand what they are trying to do or will interfere with their strong need to "do it their way". Although they dislike others imposing their will on them, they can impose their will on others. Their need for autonomy often manifests as a liking to control others and the circumstances around them. These are not co-operative people.

They have unusual ways of going about doing things, which go so far as bending the rules, for they have no problem doing things in a way that goes against common or accepted practice. They tend to act on reason and deliberate judgements, rather than on hunches or feelings; they can only be persuaded to do otherwise by logical, reasoned argument.

The Whorl on the Thumb shows someone who seeks freedom and independence so they can express who and what they are without restraint. Their individualistic nature is such that they would rather go it alone than compromise their singular integrity.

Double Loop (9–15%)

The Double Loop on the Thumb shows someone who has difficulty making up their mind or choosing a course of action. The nature of the Double Loop is such that they can always see the pros and cons of any option and may find it difficult to get sufficient clarity to make a decision. There can be much uncertainty about what to do, about which course of action to take and about their direction in life as a whole. Often, they are prone to doing one thing and wishing they'd done another, so they frequently have regrets and change their mind. As such, their aspirations are often unfulfilled either through fear of failure or because of difficulties in seeing things through due to self-doubt. They can experience confusion, uncertainty and doubt that they have done the right thing. They can feel pulled in different directions and need to see that the more useful choice lies in the ability to reconcile the differences and find a way to effect a compromise. Those with Double Loops on their Thumbs can become very good negotiators, arbitrators and mediators.

The Double Loop pattern looks very much like the *yin-yang* symbol, and it is always worth explaining that to anyone who has a Double Loop. In Western thinking we tend to see opposites as antagonistic, good versus bad, up versus down; but the *yin-yang* symbol shows us that opposites are complementary and that you can't actually have day without night or out without in. The reconciliation of opposites can be about finding a balanced compromise – or it can be finding a solution that integrates thesis with antithesis into a new synthesis. Of all the fingerprints patterns, if one can rise above the doubt and confusion, the Double Loop provides an opportunity to develop a more spiritual awareness.

Arch (3–6%)

The Arch on the Thumb shows someone who is motivated to do things with care and caution. They are likely to proceed slowly – but steadily. The Arch here adds endurance and stamina; it gives them staying power. They are more persistent and their approach is generally one of quiet determination. They apply themselves to useful tasks and dislike impractical or vague schemes. Hence, they are pragmatic decision makers, basing their decisions on practicality and a concern to get things done. They are motivated to do things that protect people or to be of service to people and are geared up to provide practical and down-to-earth assistance. In particular, they are highly motivated to do something from their innate sense of justice.

Tented Arches and *Radial Loops*

These patterns are so rarely seen here that it can be considered that they are never seen on the Thumb, certainly not with enough frequency that we can be clear as to their meaning and significance.

* * *

That covers the greater part of the dermatoglyphic patterns as they are found on each of the digits. Other patterns do sometimes occur, but generally with such infrequency that it is not possible to be sure what their significance might be. Nevertheless, now some general principles have been established, it should be a relatively easy matter to find out something of what they mean by combining together the principles of the pattern(s) involved with the qualities of the finger on which that pattern is found.

When you do find an unusual or interesting fingerprint, be open about the fact that it is unfamiliar to you and try to gain an understanding of the print by a consideration of its shape and form. This will tell you how the energy of the pattern "moves". Discuss it with your client – and then ask them to try and articulate the inner sense of the print and how it feels to have that particular fingerprint. You never know, you might make a new discovery!

Palmar Dermatoglyphics

The whole surface of the palm is covered with a fine, grain-like pattern, variously shaped and formed, and it is this grain-like pattern which forms the basis of the assessment of a hand's skin texture. But in addition to the overall roughness or smoothness of this grain, if we look carefully, we can notice particular pattern formations occurring in various parts of the palm, just as we find particular patterns on the top phalanges of each of the digits. However, unlike on the end of the fingers, it is relatively rare to find many dermatoglyphic patterns on the palm itself.

The patterns to be found on the palm are the same pattern types as we find on the digits – the Loop, the Whorl, the Arch, the Tented Arch and the Double Loop – and as with the digits, the Loop is by far the most common pattern to be found. Loops account for about 82% of all palmar patterns whereas the other pattern types that we find on the fingers make up less than 5% of the patterns to be found on the palm.

In addition to the palmar patterns proper, the palm also contains small triangular skin ridge formations known as *triradii*. These normally occur at the base of each of the fingers and in the centre at the base of the palm; there are therefore usually five triradii in each hand. Since the triradius is ruled by the Fire element, chirologically these are seen as important energisers for the finger under which they are found. Since it is most usual to have five well-placed triradii, these formations only have significance if they are absent or when they're not found where they should be.

The interpretation of the significance of palmar dermatoglyphic patterns is derived by combining the significance of the pattern type with the elemental significance of the area of the palm on which it is found. Hence, the same

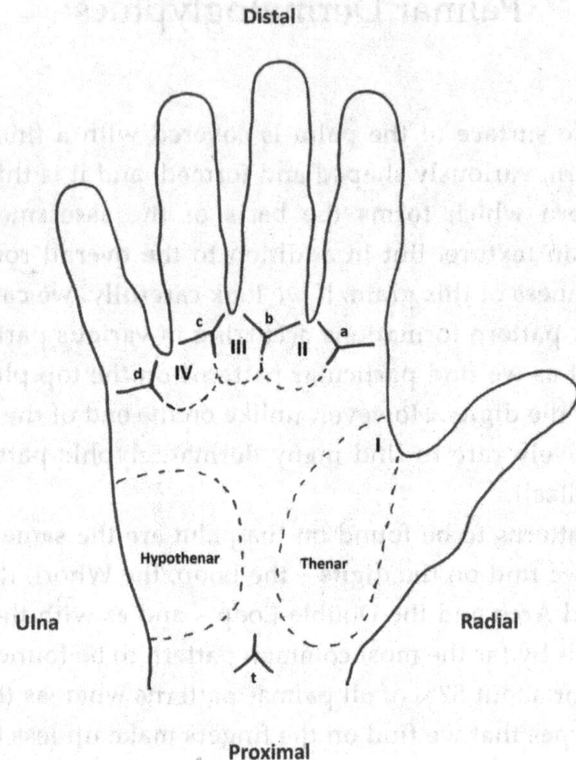

dermatoglyphic pattern has a different significance depending upon where it is located on the palm.

For the purposes of clarity, we can delineate three main areas of the palm: the Interdigital area beneath the fingers, the Thenar area of the ball of the thumb and the Hypothenar area along the ulnar side of the palm. The greatest variety of patterns occurs in the Hypothenar area of the palm, and it is here that we are most likely to find patterns other than the Loop.

The thenar area is much more likely to be without any specific patterns and so takes the form of what dermatoglyphicists call an "open field". Here the grain or flow of the skin ridges is less likely to be interrupted by the eddies of particular dermatoglyphic patterns. In fact, it is relatively common to find the whole palm an "open field", with no dermatoglyphic patterns other than the digital and axial triradii. Usually, there will be at least one palmar dermatoglyphic pattern, and most often this will be one of the Interdigital Loops. It would be rare to find a hand with four or more palmar patterns in addition to the five triradii.

Unfortunately, a plethora of names has been developed for the various palmar dermatoglyphic patterns including traditional palmistry names, elemental symbolic names and terms derived from the medical dermatoglyphic literature. The chart below also shows how frequently these patterns occur and where they occur in the palm.

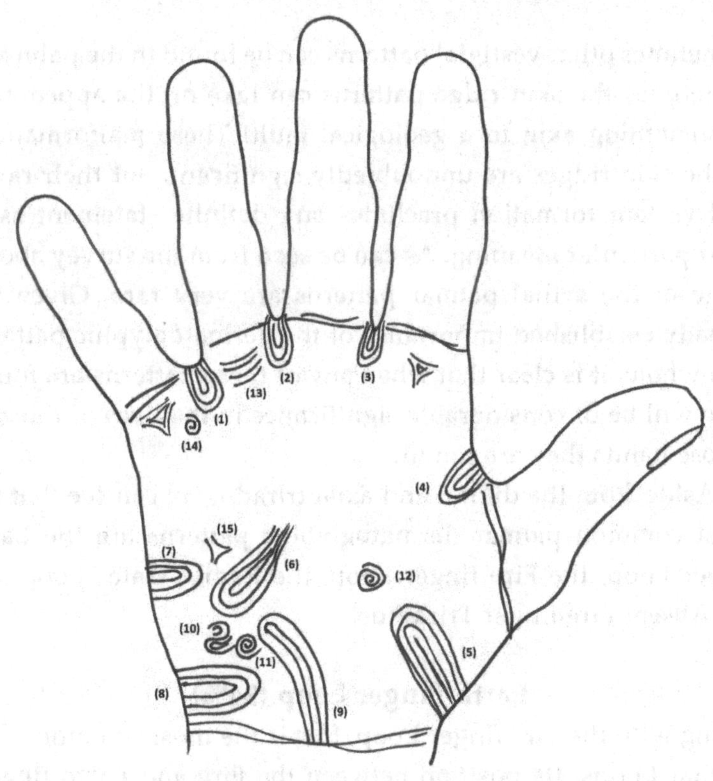

Location of the Palmar Dermatoglyphics

	Elemental/Scientific Name	Common Name	Frequency
1	Fire Finger Loop	Loop of Playfulness	35%
2	Earth Finger Loop	Loop of Seriousness	34%
3	Water Finger Loop	Loop of Leadership	4%
4	Fire Mount Loop	Loop of Courage	3%
5	Earth Mount Loop	Loop of Rhythm	4%
6	Radial Water Loop	Loop of Sensitivity	18%
7	Ulnar Water Loop	Loop of Nurture	7%
8	Lower Water Loop	Loop of Mystery	5%
9	Rising Water Loop	Loop of Inspiration	2%
10	Hypothenar Double Loop	Loop of Fluctuance	1%
11	Hypothenar Whorl	Whorl of Isolation	2%
12	Thenar Whorl	Whorl of Itinerancy	*very rare*
	Hypothenar Arch	Arch of Touch	1.6%
	Lateral Fire Finger Loop	Loop of Joy	*very rare*
13	Absent Fire Finger Triradius	Arch of Depression	11%
	Absent Air Finger Triradius	Arch of Silence	*very rare*
15	Displaced Axial Triradius	Congenital Heart Disease	4%
14	Air Interdigital Whorl	Whorl of Communication	*very rare*

Palmar Dermatoglyphic Nomenclature

Sometimes other vestigial patterns can be found in the palm and sometimes the skin ridge patterns can take on the appearance of something akin to a geological fault! These malformations of the skin ridges are undoubtedly significant, but their rarity and variant formation precludes any definite statement as to their particular meaning. As can be seen from the survey above, some of the actual palmar patterns are very rare. Given the already established importance of the dermatoglyphic patterns as a whole, it is clear that when any of these patterns are found they will be of considerable significance in the lives of those in whose hands they are found.

Aside from the digital and axial triradii, we can see that the most common palmar dermatoglyphic patterns are the Earth finger Loop, the Fire finger Loop, the Radial Water Loop and the Absent Fire finger Triradius.

Earth Finger Loop (34%)

Along with the Fire finger Loop, this is the most common of all palmar Loops. Its position between the Fire and Earth fingers reveals that it functions to unite those two energies together.

This shows that the energies of these fingers are intertwined, the more playful and creative energies of the Fire finger being contained by the more sober and serious energies of the Earth finger. For this reason, it is often referred to as the *Loop of Seriousness*.

This shows someone who takes themselves seriously; they take what they do seriously and they are generally serious about life. They are a serious person and they want to do whatever they do, seriously! They are hardworking and industrious, reliable, responsible and apply themselves assiduously to the task at hand, "If a job's worth doing, it's worth doing well!"; "We're not here to muck about; we've got work to do!" Think about a library or an accountancy office, or a law firm – very diligent, serious and hardworking environments. These people have a very well-developed Protestant work ethic.

They have a strong sense of duty and apply themselves in a concerted manner. These are the people who want to do something serious and worthwhile in their lives and are therefore concerned that they have a "proper job" with a proper salary. Their career and having some sense of progression in their career is often very important to them. *Loops of Seriousness* are commonly found in the hands of people in business and commerce, and any line of work where there must be continued application of effort over an extended period of time to become successful. These are the types who think in long-term time frames – because anything that is worthwhile will take many years to accomplish – and want to do things that have a lasting impact and produce a tangible result. Making a useful and worthwhile contribution to the world is of great importance to them. The bigger the loop, the more serious, hardworking and disciplined they are, and the stronger their ability to delay gratification. They will do things out of a sense of duty or obligation, even if they don't really want to do it.

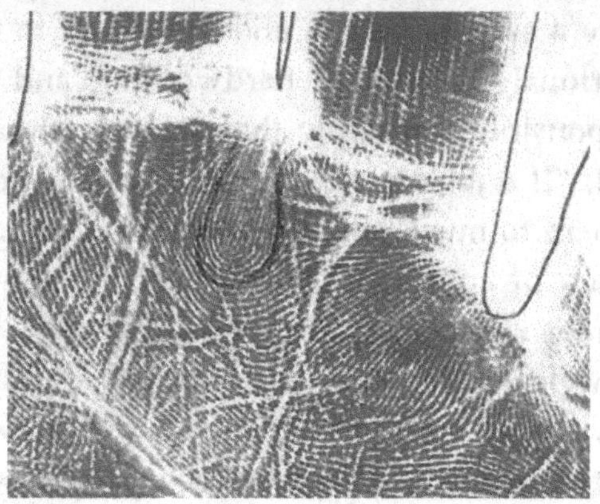

Earth Finger Loops – Loops of Seriousness

In a sense, the creativity of the person (Fire finger) is allied to the individual's sense of responsibility and duty (Earth finger) and hence they will apply their energy to more serious endeavours. They wish to use their creative energies for serious and worthwhile endeavours. They are conscientious and dependable and willing to accept responsibility. They may invest a lot of energy in attaining material or financial success. The pattern is common on people in the business world and on those who have a serious career-minded approach to life. But whatever these people actually do in their life, they do it with a certain seriousness of intent.

Fire Finger Loop (35%)

The Fire finger Loop lies between the ring finger and the little finger, and thus unites the energies represented by these two digits. Air blows on Fire, fans the flames and excites and enlivens the Fire. Hence the pattern reveals a far more light-hearted approach to life than the Earth finger Loop. These people want a life where they have fun and can enjoy themselves and this pattern is also referred to as the *Loop of Playfulness*. What this means is that they really only will do things in life that they enjoy doing. It's not that they can't work hard, but that they will only work hard if they are enjoying it, loving what they are doing. If they don't feel it, they won't do it.

Those with a *Loop of Playfulness* live more in the moment and don't think too much about the future and aren't already planning their retirement. They are far less concerned about having a stable, career-oriented life – the school Career Advisor is really only useful for those people who have *Loops of Seriousness*. Whereas the Earth finger Loop values a full-time career, the Fire finger Loop places greater value on having free time. Their view is that we work so we can live, not we live so we can work.

Whereas with a *Loop of Seriousness* the best advice is for them to find a career that they can get involved in, for those with a *Loop of Playfulness*, advise them to do what they love. These people are far more likely to get involved in lines of work that others would consider to be a hobby. Lots of artists and musicians have this loop – not that it indicates musical or artistic ability. It's just that these people are doing what they love. For those with this loop pattern, if there is a choice between two jobs and one offers more money but the other is more meaningful to them, they will choose that which is more meaningful. They are less concerned about money and status than those with *Loops of Seriousness*. They want a more flexible lifestyle, valuing enjoyment and interest in work over and above proficiency and financial reward.

Whilst it is unusual to find these together in the same hand, someone who has both the *Loop of Seriousness* and the *Loop of*

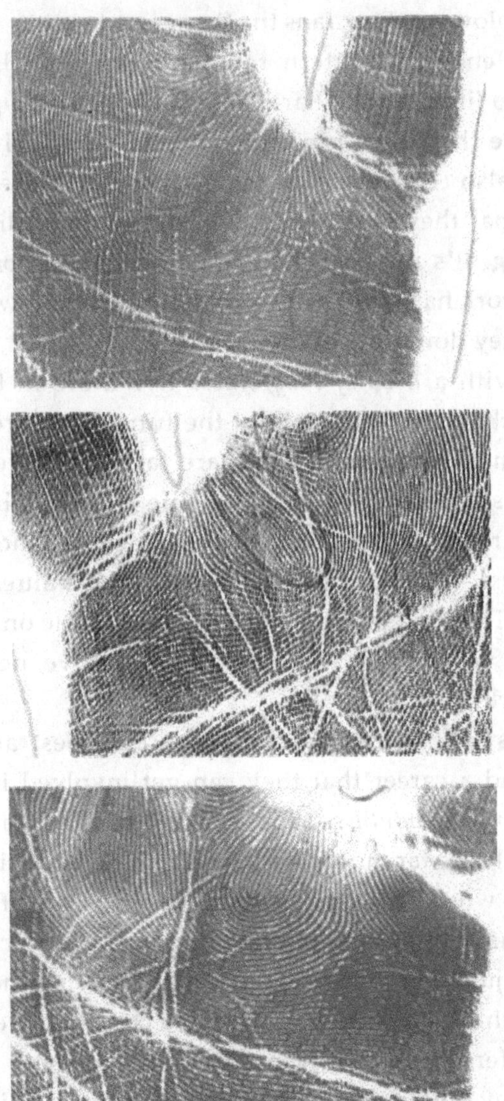

Fire finger Loop – the Loop of Playfulness

***Playfulness* needs to find something they love doing *and* take it seriously! These are the people who will make a career out of a hobby, for example.**

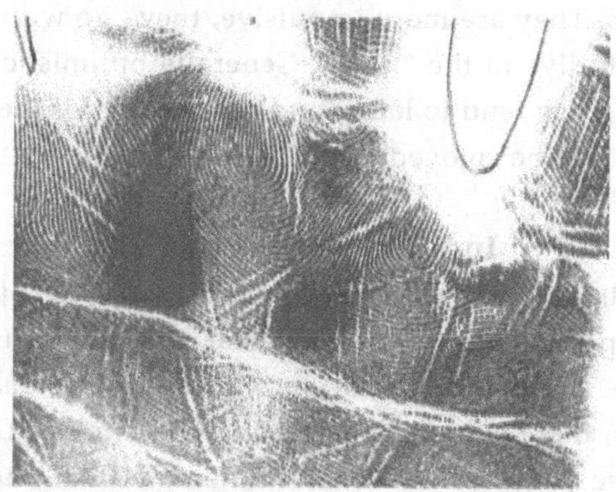

A hand with both the Loop of Playfulness and the Loop of Seriousness

Those with *Loops of Playfulness* follow their heart. If it's making their heart sing, that's the thing. There has to be passion for what they are doing; they have to feel enthusiastic about it. These people are less interested in having a high-pressure or stressful career than in doing what they enjoy. Hence, free time is very important to them as it gives them time for their other interests and activities. Consequently, they are attracted to part-time or seasonal work, or even self-employment as a means to earn the money they need to do the things that they are passionate about. Think of actors or musicians working in a bar or waitressing to pay their bills until they can earn money from what they really love doing. For these people it is most important that they enjoy whatever it is that they do – including their work. If they are working in a more conventional work space, such as an office, they will only stay there whilst it is enjoyable for them. Their workplace needs to be a fun place to be and they need to get along with the people there. If it stops being fun for them, they will leave the job and move on to a different one.

As a rule, those with this pattern have a more easy-going approach to life in general, and so like to have fun and enjoy themselves. They are more impulsive, they "go with the flow" and want to live in the "now". Generally optimistic and good humoured, they tend to laugh and smile a lot, for their attitude is that life is to be enjoyed.

Index Finger Loop (4%)

This interdigital Loop is far less common than either of the others and when present indicates a particular range of potentialities in the person. This pattern has been called the *Loop of Charisma* and oftentimes, there is indeed something charming or charismatic about these people. The boxer Muhammed Ali had one, for example. But it is important to note that charisma is not an inherent quality but more a product of the interaction between people in a particular social dynamic. Status is not a birth right, it is conferred. This pattern shows someone to whom that status is often given and these people often end up in positions of leadership within their communities. My own mother had this pattern and was a much-loved head teacher in her community school and was a leading figure in the world of education in the UK for over thirty years.

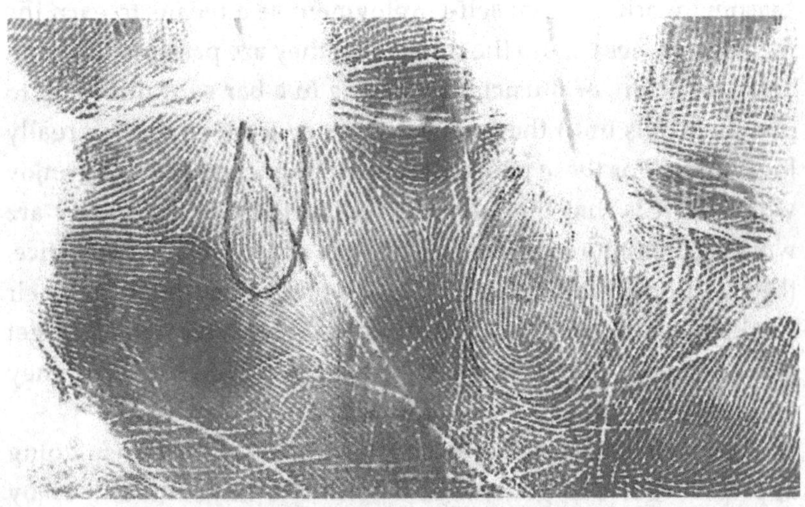

Water finger Loop and Earth finger Loop

Actually, it is more the case that this pattern shows the *potential* for leadership. Leadership is something that has to be learnt before it is earnt. Because the Loop connects the Water finger of self-identity with the authority of the Earth finger, personal authority is aligned with a strong sense of responsibility, the leadership propensity of the Water finger is lent the extra weight of authority from the Earth finger. The loop joins the two fingers together: "I want to live in accordance with my values" – so they are not preaching it but living it, role-modelling integrity and demonstrating responsible leadership. This is why this pattern reveals the ability to lead and the ability to earn respect from others.

The Maori concept of *mana* is a good concept to invoke here because *mana* is something people not only have but is something that is invested in them by the community they are in. Respect is given because of their standing in the community. They do not lead for their own glory but for the benefit of the community. They align themselves with the community.

Prominence is readily granted to these individuals as they have a natural ability to attract and command attention. This sense of assured personal authority confers executive ability and hence this pattern may be more widely found amongst professional executives and other born leaders, but also frequently amongst "gurus" or spiritual leaders. When used well, this could also be called the *Loop of Integrity* or the *Loop of Respect*. However, sometimes it is found in the hands of people who use the charisma that comes with this pattern for their own personal ends. I have seen a number of examples in recent years where people who position themselves as leaders in their communities have taken advantage of the honour bestowed on them to further their own personal financial or sexual agendas. This is a pattern of potency that needs to be handled very carefully.

Absent Ring Finger Triradius (11%)

All triradii are fire element dermatoglyphs and there are usually five triradii in the palm, one under each of the fingers and one at the centre of the base of the palm. Since four digital triradii are normally present, they have significance only if these apices are displaced or if they are entirely absent. Displacement occurs more frequently than absence. If the triradius is displaced, it combines the energies of the fingers involved. For example, the Index finger triradius offset towards the Earth finger reveals a more cautious person, whereas offset towards the Thumb side reveals a more rebellious and independent individual.

More rarely, digital triradii are actually missing. The absence of the triradius, even by itself, shows difficulties expressing the qualities of that finger. Instead of the triradius pattern, we find a collar of skin ridges forming an inverted Arch-type pattern under the finger. This suggests that the difficulty is in the form of a blockage of some kind.

The only place where the triradius is commonly absent is under the Fire finger, which occurs on more than 10% of hands and is the fourth most common palmar dermatoglyphic pattern. Beryl Hutchinson (1967) was the first to really explore the significance of this formation. She finds this to be an indication of someone who has difficulty enjoying themselves, as it seemed to her that it arrested their capacity for spontaneous self-expression. However, in my experience, I have found this pattern to indicate an awareness of a pervading sense of pessimism or sadness. Sometimes this is experienced as the recognition of a deep, dark pit, a kind of potential for deep existential crisis, into which they can easily fall if care is not taken.

Most of the people I talk to who have this pattern have experienced a deep depression in their lives at some point, the first instance often occurring around the age of 17 years. When I say to them "It's like depression... but actually it's a lot worse than that", they quietly nod and agree. They know exactly what I am referring to. It is far deeper and blacker; it is what in German is referred to as *weltschmerz*, awareness of the pain of the world. It is a deep existential sense of suffering, one that extinguishes the sense of joy from their lives. It passes, but it is a very, very difficult, dark period in their life.

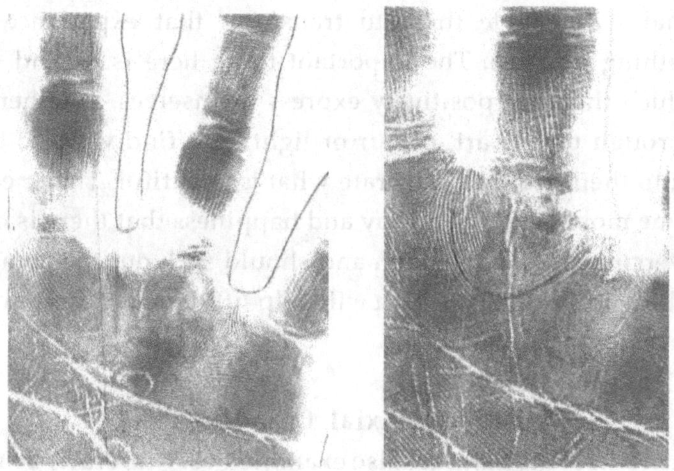

Absent Ring Finger Triradius, without and with the Traversing Line

The skin ridges align here as if to block the creative expression of the Fire finger. In some cases, this provokes the person to spend nearly all of their time in the company of others so as to almost completely avoid this deep blackness within. They are aware of it but don't want to fall into it, so set up a busy social calendar to keep things light and fun in their life. They try to keep things light; they don't want social interactions to get heavy. The effects of this dermatoglyphic pattern are often considerably mitigated if there is a line formation traversing the ridges, effectively making a bridge between the palm and the Fire finger. If this line is there, they have made a considerable effort to lift themselves out of this inner gloom. Nevertheless, they are still very much aware that this pit of darkness is not always too far beneath the surface.

It is therefore important for these people to find some form of artistic or creative expression. The Fire finger is all about joy, fun, socialising, parties – and all of these activities will go some way to alleviate the sense of darkness. But the best remedy of all is for them to learn how to express themselves creatively and artistically, whichever form of art they can do that through, as that will enable them to transform that experience into something positive. The important thing here is to find ways in which they can positively express themselves, whether that be through music, art, colour or light, and find ways to bring joy into their life, and celebrate what is beautiful. They need to become more aware of the joy and happiness that there is in life to overcome this disposition and should seek out the company of others or situations which will help lift them out from within themselves.

Displaced Axial Triradius (4%)

The triradii of the palm are also examined very carefully by those engaged in genetic research and medical dermatoglyphics. Here, the digital triradii are labelled from A to D and the axial triradius is labelled T. The angle formed by connecting triradius A with T, and D with T is known as the ATD angle,

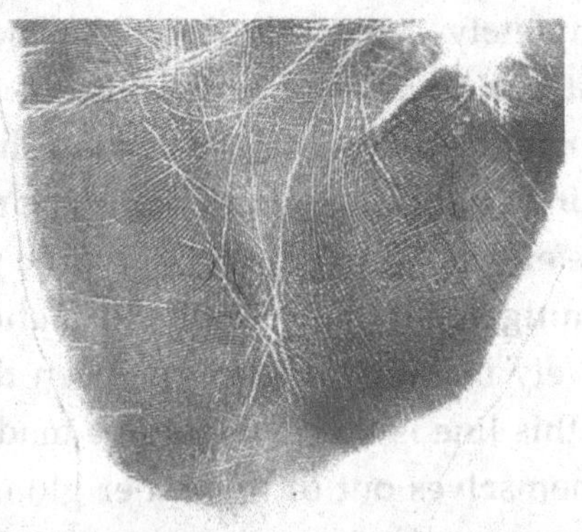

Displaced Axial Triradius

and when the axial triradius is normally located at the base of the palm, the ATD angle is around 45 degrees. However, sometimes the axial triradius can be considerably displaced. When it is displaced to a point much higher in the palm, such that the ATD angle increases to around 60 degrees or more, this is widely regarded by many dermatoglyphicists as being a significant indication of genetic abnormality. The displaced axial triradius is extremely common in Down Syndrome and the research of LS Penrose and others has indicated that it is the most potent indicator of the likelihood that a person will produce a Down Syndrome child.

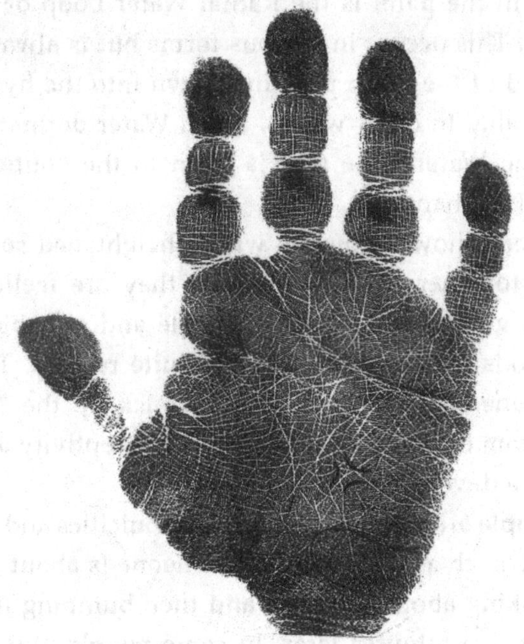

Displaced Axial Triradius in Down Syndrome

According to the findings of other medical dermatoglyphic research, this displacement also occurs with much greater frequency in people with congenital heart weakness – and it is worth noting here that the majority of people with Down

Syndrome are also born with congenital heart defects. Whilst a cardiac diagnosis should always take other factors into consideration, for example, the condition of the nails and the fingertips, people with this pattern should be advised to have proper medical examinations at regular intervals. Remember, the pattern is not so much an indication of heart disease as of congenital heart weakness. People with this pattern can experience poor peripheral circulation as well.

Radial Water Loop (18%)

Proximal to the digital mount area, the most common pattern to be found in the palm is the Radial Water Loop or the *Loop of Sensitivity*. This occurs in various forms but is always found with the head of the Loop pointing down into the hypothenar area of the palm. In other words, it is a Water dermatoglyphic pattern in the Water zone that is open to the "outside", the radial side of the hand.

This pattern shows someone with a heightened sensitivity, particularly to other people and how they are feeling. They sense what's going on with other people and are able to pick up their moods and emotional states quite readily. They also are highly tuned to environments and pick up the "vibe" or "feel" of a room or place. This heightened receptivity also often manifests as a developed "sixth sense".

These people are often aware of synchronicities and uncanny coincidences, such as knowing that someone is about to phone them or thinking about someone and then bumping into them on the street five minutes later. In some people, this can also manifest as a strong awareness of their dreams, which in some cases can even be prophetic. Learning to pay attention to their dreams is a good way for them to develop their intuitive abilities as, along with using tarot cards or other oracular tools, it will facilitate the development of more magical and symbolic ways of seeing the world.

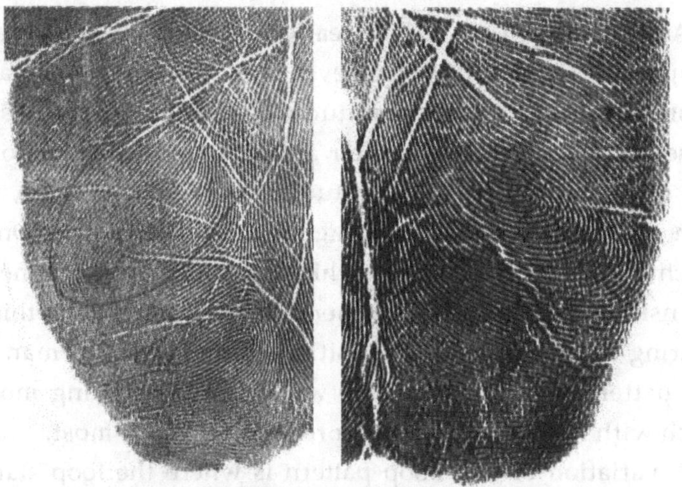

Radial Water Loop or Loop of Sensitivity

In general, this pattern denotes what is referred to as a psychic awareness or a potential psychic ability. I consider it an indicator of an ability to tune into the "energy field" that exists around all animate life which, if listened to, can give a degree of intuitive or precognitive ability. This can be especially pronounced if the Air line terminates deep into the core of the Loop or if there is a strong, long and clear Minor Air line, a combination which is often seen in the hands of tarot readers, clairvoyants and mediums. In a study I conducted in 1992 of the hands of those actively pursuing the development of psychic abilities, this pattern was found at a much higher incidence (45%) than amongst the general population (18%).

One thing that should be noted is that this pattern is a form of *Radial Loop*, which is to say it shows a sensitivity to picking things up from the external environment and the people around them, as does a digital Radial Loop. The difference is that being in the palm, this intuitive sensing is felt within the body – people often report that they experience the hairs go up on the back of their neck or they get an aching in their knees, or a shiver-shake down their spine. Others will describe their intuition as a "gut feeling". It is fair to describe this loop pattern as a body-based energic sensor.

As a pattern in itself, it really only shows the potential for psychic receptivity. However, people with this pattern presumably have a greater aptitude for learning such skills than those without it. Whether their abilities are developed or not will often depend on their attitude towards such things, since such abilities are often disparaged, if not dismissed. On less psychically developed people, this pattern shows someone who is sensitive and receptive to others and thus gives something of a caring or sympathetic disposition. For example, a man with this pattern in his Water zone will be seen as being more in touch with his emotions and more sensitive than most.

A variation of this Loop pattern is where the loop starts to form in the centre of the palm as the ridges start diverging, but they don't come back together. Actually, they do – but the apex point of the Loop is actually *off* the palm. I have found this "open-ended" Loop or "Psychic Awareness Field" pattern in the hands of strikingly psychic persons, shamans and channelers. They report being able to communicate with other realms.

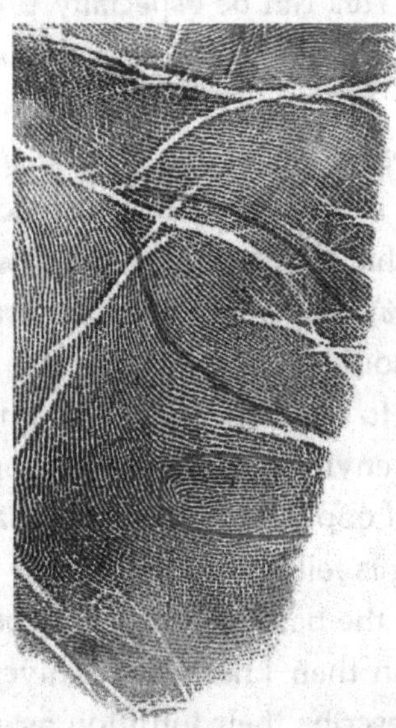

Psychic Awareness Field

Ulnar Water Loop (7%)

A second Loop pattern to occur in the hypothenar area is the Ulnar Water Loop, but here the Loop opens from the percussion edge of the palm under the Little finger and points out towards the Thumb. Here again, there is an increased sensitivity, but this time one that is directed towards things of the earth or towards the earth's energies.

Sometimes called the *Loop of Nature,* this pattern shows a strong affinity with plants and animals and can give a strong interest in gardening, horticulture and growing things. The pattern is common in the hands of those with Down Syndrome, which suggests a good range of activities for them to get involved in. People with a *Loop of Nature* are suited to living in the countryside or doing work that involves the earth in some way, e.g., animal husbandry, having a small farm or doing landscape gardening. There is a deep love of nature and the natural world. Nurturing animals and the natural environment is a skill that comes naturally to them. If they are urban dwellers, getting out into nature is of considerable importance to them. These people also have the proverbial "green fingers"

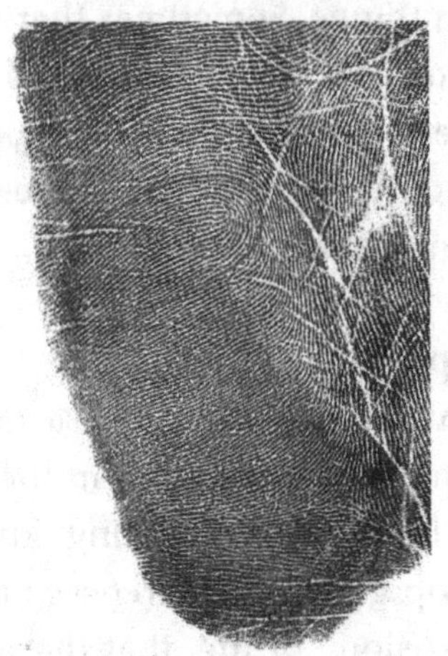

Ulnar Water Loop

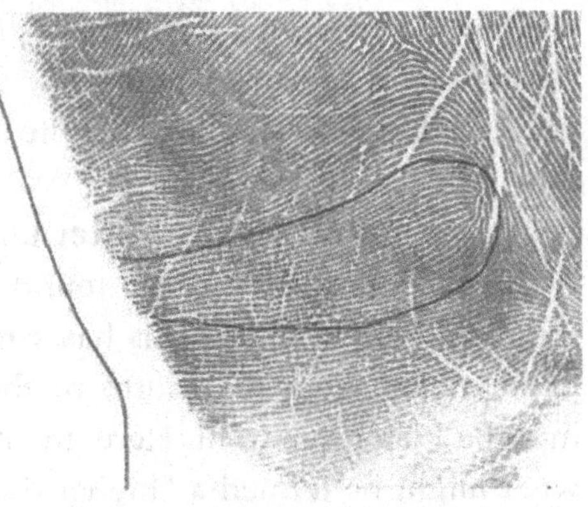

Lower Water Loop

and often make keen horticulturists – if only in their spare time. The pattern gives a natural feel for the earth and can indicate a gift for sensing vibrations in places and objects, such as ley lines and stone circles. One woman I know with this pattern travels the world persuading governments to establish 30% of their waters as marine reserves in an attempt to preserve the natural aquatic environments of their local ocean.

Lower Water Loop (5%)

This Loop pattern is similar in formation to the Ulnar Water Loop except that it occurs much lower down in the palm, at the base of the Water zone and is sometimes referred to as the *Loop of Mystery*. This pattern in seen in the hands of those with an interest in things like astrology, tarot cards, mystery religions, Wicca, karma, rebirth and reincarnation, near-death experiences and depth psychology. They are fascinated by what goes on beneath the surface and want to know and understand the deeper forces at work within human experiences. There is often an innate urge to get to the root of things and uncover the hidden laws that govern life itself. This can manifest as a desire to study esoteric philosophies or the occult for there is a fascination with or a love of mysteries and hidden things. Sometimes there may simply be an interest in detection and detective stories. However it manifests, this pattern gives an interest in all things mysterious or somehow hidden and underground for it indicates a fascination with all things that lie beneath the surface.

Rising Water Loop (2%)

A third Loop pattern to be found in the hypothenar area is the Rising Water Loop. This has a more central location in the palm, rising from the centre of the hand and extending up into the Water quadrant. Here, the Loop gives an awareness of what might be termed a "higher dimension" of life, that there is some realm beyond what is apparent, that there is a hidden reality beyond that which is ordinarily seen. This pattern can be found on generally artistic individuals or people who derive great inspiration from art, such as an art historian. In particular, this pattern occurs in the hands of artists and musicians and often suggests great musical or artistic talent. The loop acts as a source of inspiration; inspiration bursts into their consciousness from some undefinable higher or inner source. One of the most talented and innovative jazz guitarists I know has this formation as does a late-blooming artist friend who became an inspirational painter in her 60s. Otherwise, the pattern can indicate that they are somewhat mystically inclined and have a fine appreciation of otherworldly dimensions, whether that is inspired by art, music, religion or psychedelic substances. There is a desire to know "that which is beyond" the immediacy of the everyday world. In some cases, this gives a strong interest in what are commonly referred to as conspiracy theories. Other factors in the hand would need to be considered to determine which of these it would be.

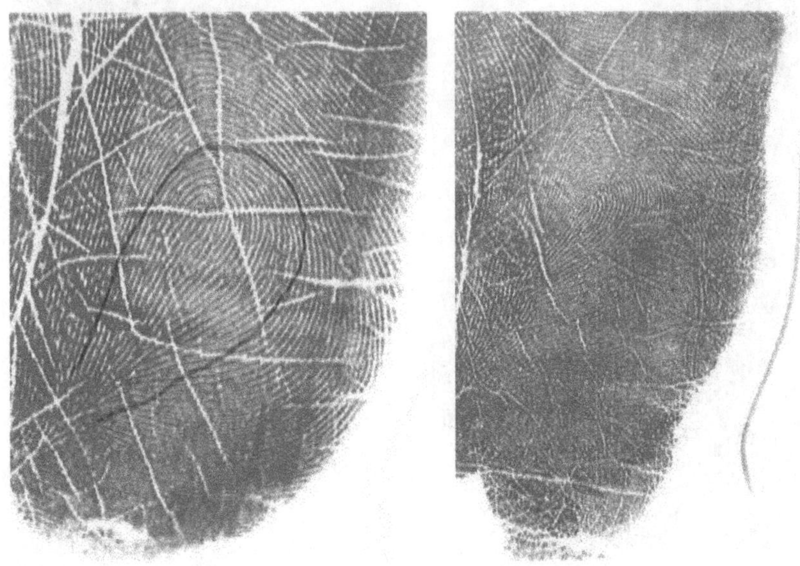

Rising Water Loops

Fire Mount Loop (3%)

The Fire Mount Loop is located on the upper thenar area of the hand where the Thumb joins the radial edge of the palm. In palmistry books we find this pattern referred to as the *Loop of Courage*. With this pattern, there can be a strong love of sport or a fascination with activities like martial arts and body building. There can be an intense love of excitement or an obsession with the thrill of the adrenalin rush such that sometimes people with this pattern deliberately put themselves into situations of physical danger. They may like to participate in dangerous sports or other activities with an element of risk, such as rock climbing or swimming with sharks. One recent example that I encountered was in the hands of a helicopter rescue pilot, someone who intentionally put himself in dangerous situations to rescue others! It can be an indicator of someone who embraces physical courage and fearlessness.

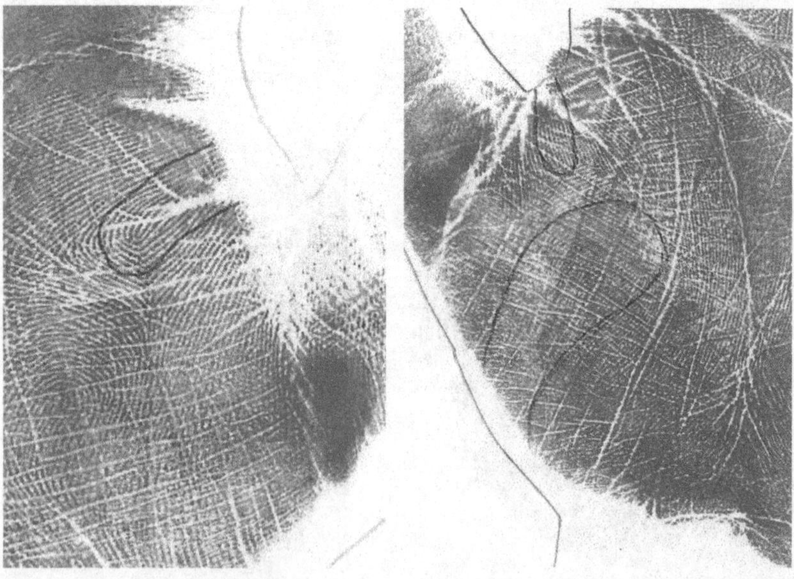

Fire Mount Loop **Fire Mount and Earth Mount Loops**

Whilst this pattern can be an indication of courageousness, I think it rather indicates a kind of fearlessness. A diminutive female television producer that I know had no fear in going to Los Angeles to make a documentary about the street gangs there or interviewing IRA terrorists, despite the possible dangers. As with many of the other palmar dermatoglyphic patterns, the manifestations of this pattern in people's lives can be quite varied and other features of the hand need to be considered to show you where this disposition will find expression. In general, a Loop here inclines the person to adopt an attitude of courage and fearlessness. As a consequence, they like to set themselves challenges, whether those challenges be physical or mental, in order to prove, at least to themselves, that this fear can be overcome.

It's notable that when there is a *Loop of Courage*, oftentimes there is also a *Loop of Rhythm*.

Earth Mount Loop (4%)

The Earth Mount Loop is located on the thenar side of the hand, rising from the base of the palm in a similar manner to the

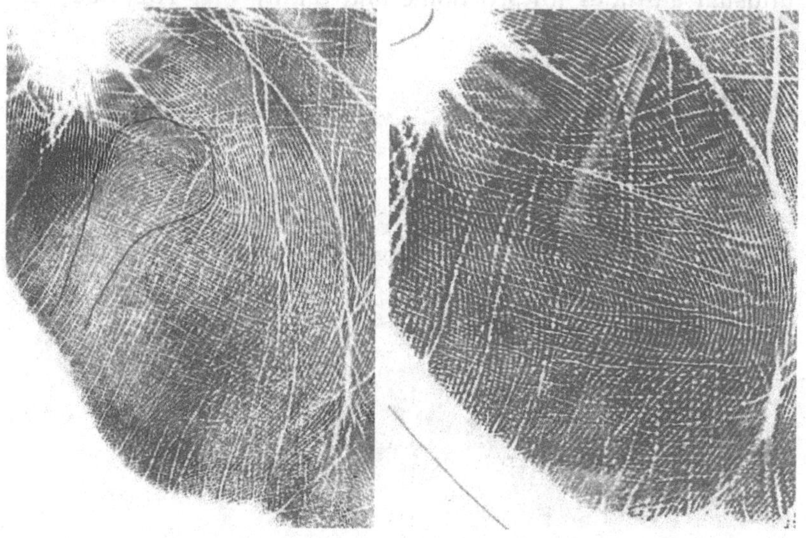

Earth Mount Loops

Rising Water Loop. Here too, the Loop reveals a strong interest in and appreciation of music, but unlike the Rising Water Loop it does not necessarily reveal any musical talent or ability. Sometimes called the *Loop of Rhythm*, the Earth Mount Loop reveals someone who has a strong love of music and the effect it has on them. All kinds of music and all kinds of rhythms have a powerful effect on their consciousness but particularly things like reggae, electronic dance music, African drumming, Japanese *Taiko* drumming, Latin American salsa or other forms of overtly percussive music. Often seen in the hands of Pacific Islanders, these are people who are powerfully moved by music, are incredibly responsive to the pulse of the beat and have a strong love of dance and dancing. They need to get up and move!

Thenar Whorl (<1%)

A Whorl in the Earth area of the hand suggests there will be something usual or different about their lifestyle or living arrangements, earth being related to home. They will have unusual attitudes toward home and family life. They may, for

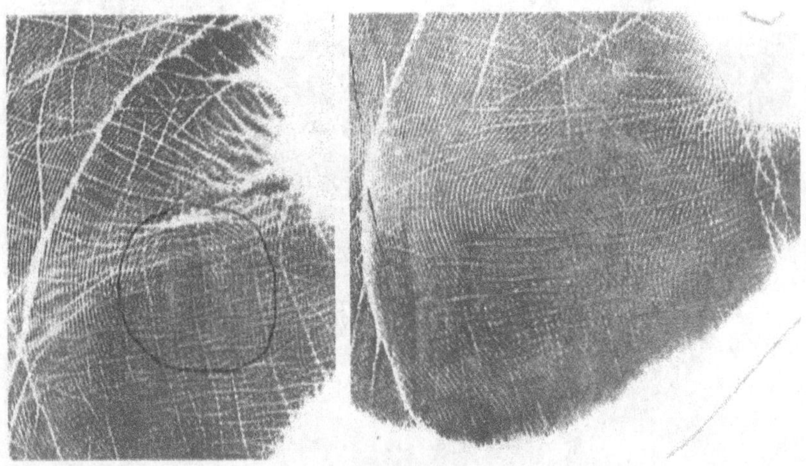

Thenar Whorl

example, be drawn to the idea of living in a bus or a house truck or on a narrowboat, in other words a house that moves! They want freedom in the area of the home and have a desire to see the world. The pattern suggests that their basic life-values are indeed different in some way, and they are more likely to have a travelling and itinerant lifestyle.

Hypothenar Whorl (2%)

A Whorl in the hypothenar area of the hand can be a troubling and difficult experience for the person who has this pattern. Essentially what the Whorl suggests here is emotional isolation, a contained emotional experience that creates unusual emotional experiences. If you see this pattern the first thing to ask of them is if they feel trapped "inside" the whorl or whether they feel there is a "secret, hidden part of themselves" which is somehow deep and inaccessible. Or are they "outside" the whorl, with that pattern suggesting an isolated part of their consciousness, a private, secret, hidden self or source that they are aware of but that is unseen by others. Those with this pattern can have the

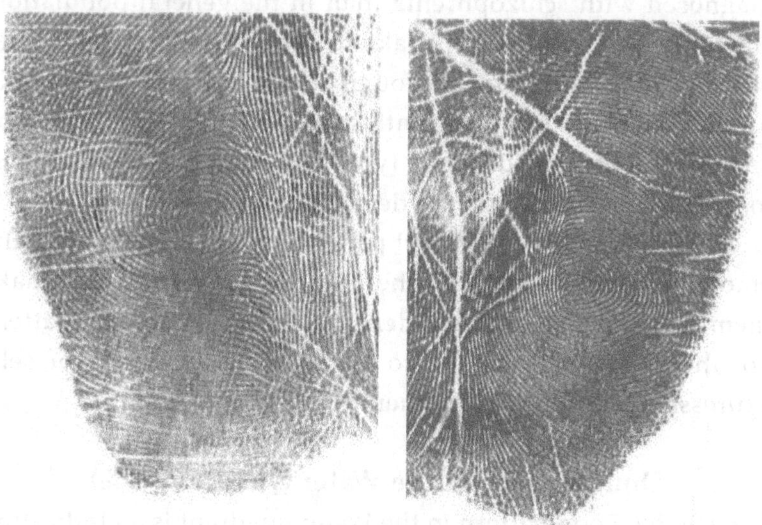

Hypothenar Whorl

experience of having had a difficult childhood where they felt like they were living in a bubble and could not reach out or get across to others. As a result, they may be acutely conscious of a unique and differentiated inner self. Loneliness and alienation can be an acute part of their experience.

Others who are more aware of this pattern are aware of a part of themselves which is a source of rich creativity. By itself, the pattern merely shows that the person may be self-contained and have a penchant for working alone. But it is also true that those with a Whorl on this part of the hand can be very artistic and creative and it is this aspect that is worth emphasising when you come across a hand with this pattern.

The noted singer/musician Annie Lennox has such a pattern in her right hand and has often spoken of her mental health issues, including that she has suffered agoraphobia and severe depression. She has also talked about how she has recognised that some of her best artistic work came out of these struggles.[1]

Medical dermatoglyphic studies have found Whorls are in fact more common in the hypothenar area of the hand in those diagnosed with schizophrenia than in the general population. However, it would be a mistake to associate this pattern with schizophrenia *per se* for although it may be more commonly found in the hands of those with schizophrenia, it is likely to be an indicator of many different types of mental health conditions, including conditions such as depression or agoraphobia.

Psychologically, the Whorl pattern here tends to *contain* the emotional consciousness of the individual, and this can make them feel isolated or misunderstood. Those with this pattern are therefore well advised to develop artistic forms of self-expression, even if only for therapeutic purposes.

Double Loop in the Water Quadrant (1%)

The Double Loop pattern in the Water quadrant is an indication of someone who feels things very deeply and very strongly.

The pattern creates an internal emotional turbulence which is difficult for the person to ignore. Their feelings oscillate intensely between various emotions and there can be a lot of emotional instability in their life, and often difficulties in their emotional relationships with others because of this. In many cases, these feelings will be buried; they will keep a lid on how they really feel about things because this pattern can be psychologically very destabilising. They can experience much inner emotional turmoil and confusion which sometimes reflects a desire to experiment with their emotional and sexual identity. They feel things in opposite extremes, but holding back how they feel is very difficult and won't feel "right" and will eventually come out. For example, this pattern is sometimes seen in the hands of those who go through gender reassignment. It is interesting to note in this respect that the Double Loop pattern here has been found by medical dermatoglyphicists to be more common amongst those with conditions such as Turner's and Klinefelter's Syndromes, suggesting a link between this pattern and sex chromosome anomalies.

One evident characteristic is that men with this pattern are more in tune with how they feel than most men. Women with this pattern in their hand can have a more masculine build and

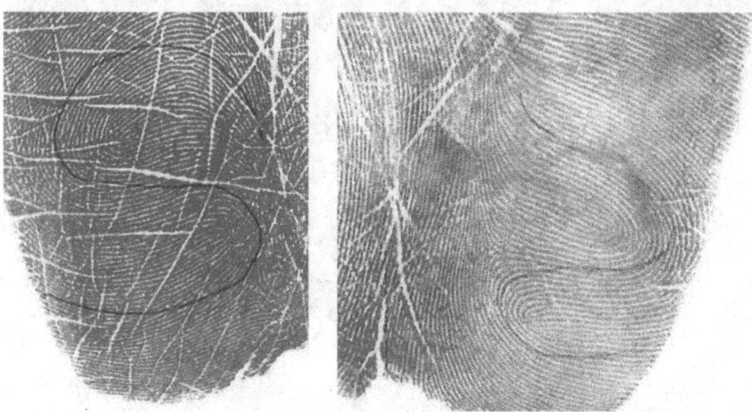

Double Loop in the Hypothenar Area

demeanour. I have met women with this pattern who were tough, hard business negotiators and who were very successful in the business world. However, another woman I know with this pattern is an ambient music DJ and she creates woven tapestries of flowing sound textures on the dancefloor. The location of the pattern in the palm is a reflection of how the music pulses through her body. In a man I know, he is a very sensitive professional jazz musician. In all cases, there is a more profound awareness of the fluctuations of feelings and a greater emotional sensitivity. What they do with that and how it affects them will be seen by looking at other features of the hands.

Hypothenar Arch (1.6%)

An Arch pattern running through the Water area of the hand reveals a certain emotional reticence and reserve and there can be a sense of sadness and loneliness about them because of this. Essentially, this pattern gives a practical, "down to earth" emotional expression with a strong tactile component. They

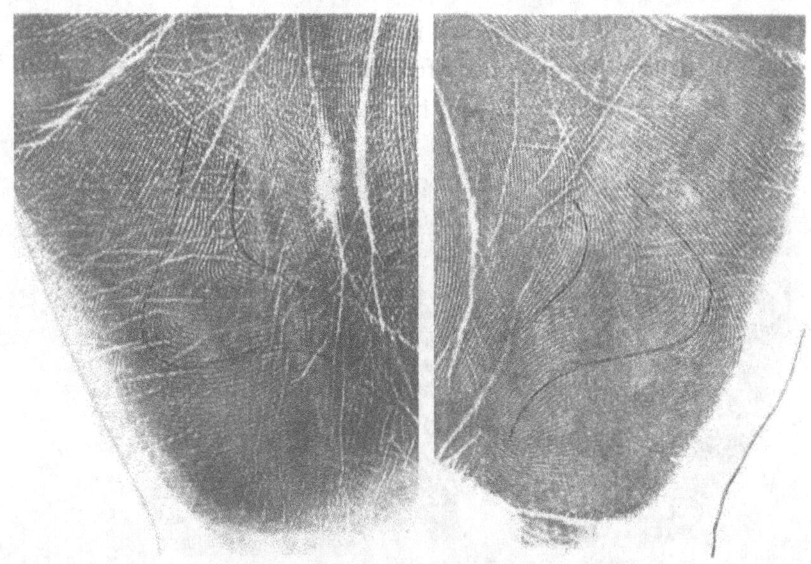

Arch in the Hypothenar Area

understand that physical touch is more about the emotional connection that touch provides, rather than just physical contact.

People with this pattern find it easier to express themselves emotionally through touch and hugging. Physical contact is important for their emotional sense of wellbeing and they believe in the importance of touch in conveying their feelings to others. This makes them natural mothers and nurturers so it is unsurprising that this pattern can be seen in those who care for the bodily needs of others, such as those working with children or in the care of the elderly. The pattern can also be seen in the hands of massage and body work therapists, expressing care and concern for another in a patently tactile manner.

Lateral Fire Finger Loop (<1%)

This is a variation of the *Loop of Playfulness* but here the loop lies more horizontally across the palm and runs *under* the ring finger. As this finger relates to our persona and personal image, so the loop here augments and enhances the person's dress sense, sense of aesthetics and sense of beauty, art and colour. It can therefore show someone who has a distinctive and colourful style of dress. They are conscious of what they wear and they like to wear things that are colourful and bright, because they like to bring colour, light and joy. Their highly developed sense of colour and appreciation of beauty may also give them an eye for interior design, home décor or making beautifully designed gardens full of colour and speckled with art.

I have named this pattern the *Loop of Joy* or *Loop of Exuberance* as it often manifests as a desire to dress up in colourful outfits or costumes, someone who has an eccentric and colourful presentation or who can be a "snazzy dresser". They are not so much dressing up and putting something on – rather, they are bringing something out from within. Their flamboyance is a form of expression. Not a show, but an expression of who they are, not a costume but a manifestation of their inner state. It is not

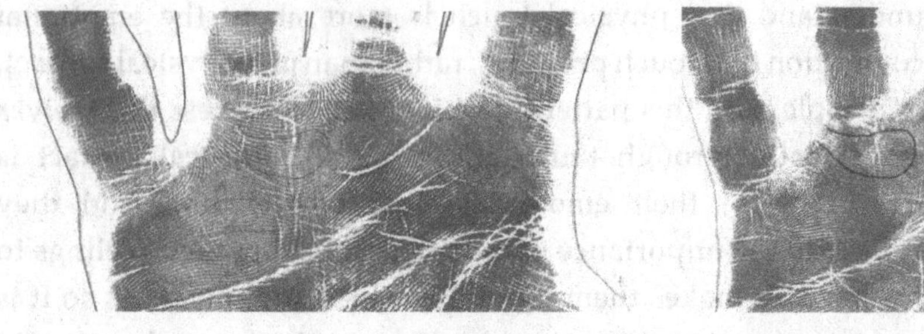

Loop of Joy

vanity, as Beryl Hutchinson first suggested, even if the outfits themselves are extraordinary. Rather, it is a manifestation of a strong desire to bring colour and joy into the world and bring a smile to people's faces.

Interdigital Whorls (<1%)

Whorl patterns at the base of the fingers are extremely rare. Beneath the ring finger, an interdigital Whorl can give something original or distinctive with regard to the way in which they dress or present themselves. If found under the Air (little) finger, which is a little bit more common, it indicates that there is something quite unusual or distinctive about the way the person thinks and gives a unique quality of originality to their communication. It is a pattern that is seen on highly intelligent and gifted people. I have seen it on the hands of people who are musically talented and people with an exceptional talent for languages. One Croatian woman I know with this pattern is an exceptional linguist – fluent in English and German, she has translated Chinese and Japanese Buddhist texts into *English*! Another woman is good at finding original ways of communicating with people with learning difficulties. A singer-songwriter I know has a strikingly penetrating insight into the human condition. Through her poetic use of words, her singing brings her audiences to tears.

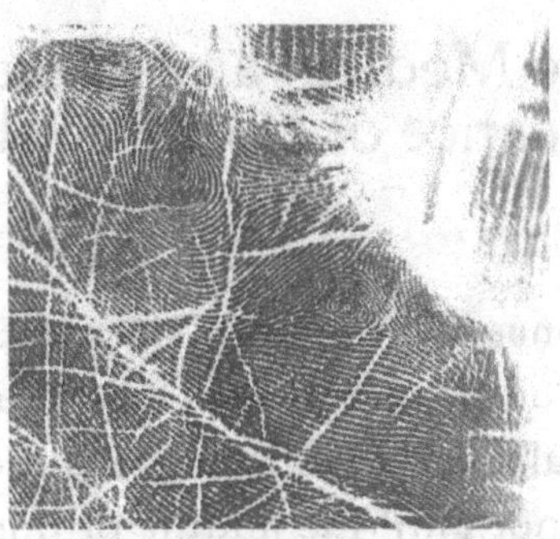

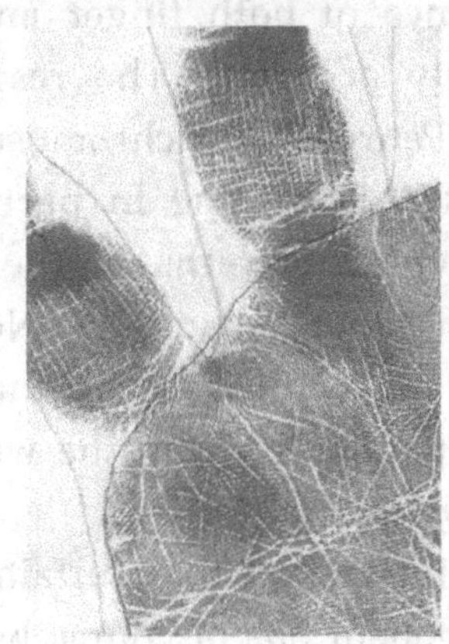

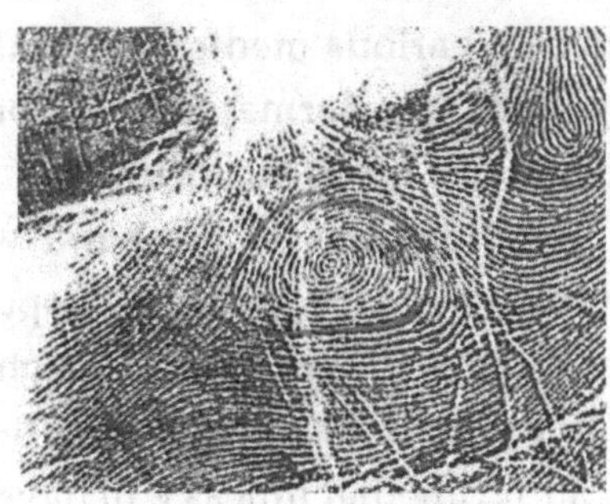

Interdigital Whorls

---

1. **"Lennox said she had bad bouts of depression living in Aberdeen and blamed it on the city's dreary climate. But depression has been a lifelong struggle for Lennox.... Depression continued as she became an adult, and Lennox soon realized what many artists do: her best work came from despondency." https://www.grunge.com/1083273/ tragic-details-about-annie-lennox/**

The Medical and Genetic Significance of Dermatoglyphics

Ever since the pioneering work of Galton in the late nineteenth century, it has been recognised that the dermatoglyphic patterns of the palm are of immense significance genetically. However, it was not until the middle of this century that the diagnostic significance of both finger and palmar patterns became more widely accepted. The research of Cummins and Midlo and LS Penrose into chromosomal abnormalities in general and Down Syndrome in particular have shown that the dermatoglyphic patterns of the palm are reliable indicators of certain genetic disorders. Noel Jaquin has also shown something of the medical significance of the fingerprint patterns, quite independently from the work of Penrose and other medical geneticists.

Since that time, the notion that certain medical disorders have a genetic component has of course become more widely accepted, and by 1974, three and a half thousand or more papers had been published in various medical journals conveying the results of investigations into dermatoglyphic patterns and their correlations with specific medical disorders. A consideration of the dermatoglyphic patterns of the hand will thus furnish us with some indications of hereditary dispositions towards certain disease conditions. Clearly though, such indications will only reveal a tendency towards certain conditions; whether the person is actually suffering that illness will have to be confirmed by other features of the hand.

However, whilst it is true that the dermatoglyphics cannot change in terms of their pattern from the fourth month of gestation – hence their genetic significance – they *can* change in terms of their quality. We shall have the opportunity to consider these dermatoglyphic phenomena more fully later. In the meantime, we should start by considering the general genetic significance of dermatoglyphic patterns.

Fingerprint Patterns

Of the seven main types of fingerprint patterns, six have been associated with genetic dispositions to various health disorders. The first suggestions of correlations between fingerprint pattern types and health disorders were made by Noel Jaquin in the 1930s; many of his observations have subsequently been confirmed fifty or more years later by scientific dermatoglyphic researchers. The number of a specific type of fingerprint pattern present in the hands is especially important given that fingerprint patterns vary enormously in their distributions, as we have seen. Three Arches can be considered to be sufficient to be indicative of a genetic predisposition to its associated disorders whereas five Whorls, two Double Loops, two Tented Arches and nine or ten Loops are needed to be indicative of a genetic disposition to the disorders related to these patterns. The more there are of a certain fingerprint pattern type, the greater the likelihood of a disposition towards those disorders.

Arch – The presence of three or more Arches denotes a genetic disposition towards intestinal and digestive disorders, particularly constipation, pseudo-intestinal obstruction, spastic colon and other conditions of chronic intestinal pain.

Ulnar Loops – These are perhaps too common to be specific indicators, unless they occur on nine or more digits. In this number they give an enhanced susceptibility to immune dysfunction and impairment of the nervous system. Nerve trouble (e.g., neuritis), Alzheimer's disease and pre-senile dementia have all been associated with the presence of high numbers of Loops. Clearly, afflictions to the nervous system can cause impairments to the functioning of the mind. Large numbers of Ulnar Loops are extremely common in Down Syndrome, which itself gives a predisposition to degenerative mental conditions such as Alzheimer's and pre-senile dementia.

Double Loops – These are associated with the development of conditions such as auto-toxaemia within the body. Three or more patterns would be needed to suggest a disposition to these disorders, especially if they are found on digits other than the Thumb.

Tented Arches – These are associated with a highly strung and highly sensitive nervous system and a predisposition to disorders of the nervous system. Two or more Tented Arches can be considered to be sufficient here. Tented Arches have also been found to be five times more common in the hands of schizophrenics than in the general population.

Whorls – Whorls are associated with intensity of lifestyle and hence stress conditions that may affect the functioning of the heart. There is considerable dermatoglyphic evidence to suggest a specific link between the presence of Whorls and certain types of heart disease, especially where more than five Whorls are found. Eye weaknesses and sight defects such as myopia or photosensitivity have also been associated with increased numbers of Whorls.

Radial Loop – The Radial Loop is most usually found on the Index finger, if found at all, and is almost never found on other fingers in the general population. However, in chromosomal disorders such as Down Syndrome, Edwards Syndrome and Patau Syndrome, Radial Loops can be found more frequently on the ring finger or even the little finger. This pattern is virtually never found here otherwise, and so is taken by some dermatoglyphicists to be a general indication of a chromosomal anomaly.

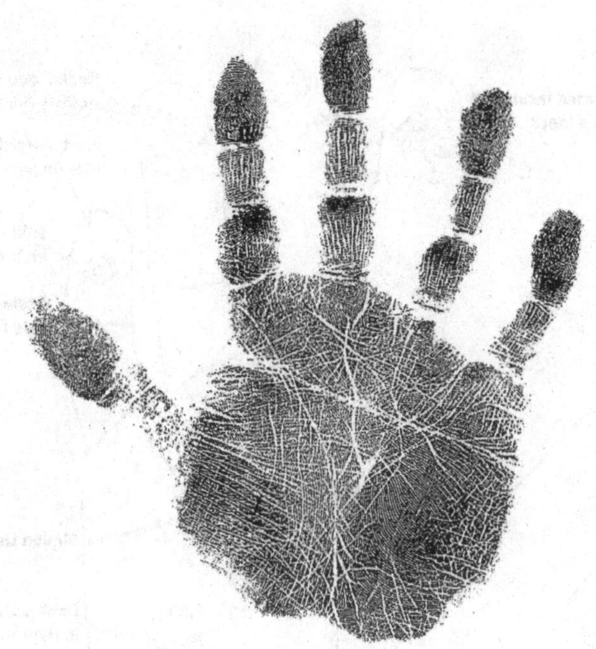

Simian line and missing inter-phalangeal crease on the Little finger

Medical Dermatoglyphic Discoveries

The following diseases, conditions and syndromes have been studied by dermatoglyphic researchers over the last 100 years:

Congenital Heart Defects – Heart defects may be indicated by the presence of a Simian line but are most conspicuously indicated by a displaced axial triradius such that the ATD angle is fifty-seven degrees or more. This has been found to be present in all types of congenital heart conditions. Note that the displaced axial triradius is also extremely common in people with Down Syndrome, who are frequently born with congenital heart defects that are very often the cause of their early demise.

Leukaemia – Certain types of leukaemia have been associated with an increased incidence of the Sydney line: an Air line which traverses the palm right across to the ulnar edge, indicative of excess air.

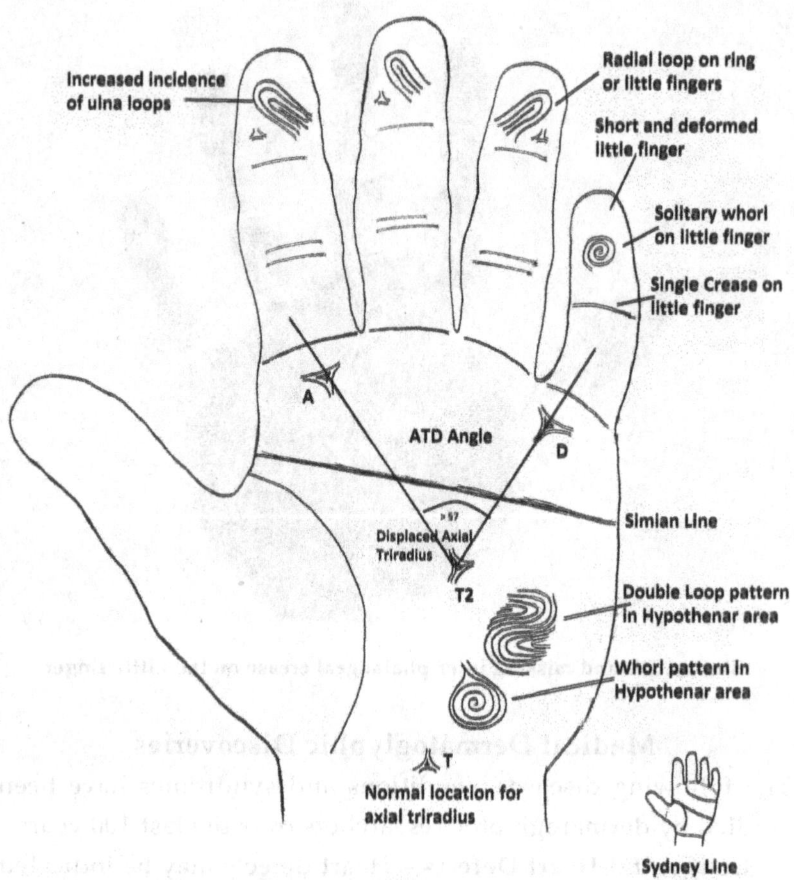

Medical Dermatoglyphic discoveries in the Hand

Congenital Cognitive Impairment – The single crease on the Little finger is very common in those congenital disorders which produce severe intellectual disability and hence may be indicative of learning disabilities and low IQ. This formation is also common in Down Syndrome.

Down Syndrome – Dermatoglyphically this is characterised by a displaced axial triradius, increased incidence of Ulnar Loops and increased incidence of Radial Loops on fingers other than the Index finger. However, other hand features are also of importance here. The hands tend to be broad and short with stumpy fingers and the Little finger is often short and bent toward the Ring finger. Frequently the Little finger only has one interphalangeal crease, despite having three bony phalanges. The Thumb tends to be short and high-set and, in addition, over fifty per cent of those with Down Syndrome have a Simian line.

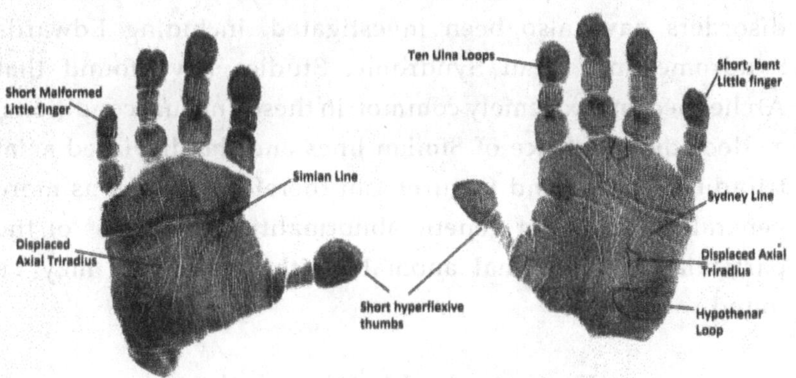

Common Hand Features Seen in Down Syndrome

Displaced Axial Triradius – 85% of cases had t^2 displacement
Simian Line – 55% cases have at least one Simian line
Ulnar Loops – 83% of fingerprint patterns
Ten Ulnar Loops – occurs in 35% cases (~4% in general pop^n)
Short & Bent Little fingers – 55% cases (~2% in general pop^n)
Missing Phalangeal Crease – 26% cases have a crease missing on the Little finger

Schizophrenia – An increased incidence of Whorls in the Water quadrant in the hands of schizophrenics has been found as a significant indicator of an inherited disposition towards this condition. Whorls here give a sense of emotional isolation or alienation. Also, increased numbers of Tented Arch fingerprints have been found in the hands of schizophrenics.

Sex Chromosome Disorders – These are associated with an increased incidence of solitary Whorls or other unusual dermatoglyphic patterns on the Little finger. Studies have also ascertained that conditions such as Klinefelter's Syndrome tend to produce an increased incidence of Double Loop composite patterns in the hypothenar area of the palm.

Other Chromosomal Disorders – Many other chromosomal disorders have also been investigated, including Edwards Syndrome and Patau Syndrome. Studies have found that Arches become extremely common in these unusual conditions, as does the incidence of Simian lines and the displaced axial triradius. These hand features can therefore be seen as more general indicators of genetic abnormalities regardless of the particular chromosomal anomaly with which they may be found.

Dermatoglyphic Dissociation

Whilst dermatoglyphics cannot change in terms of their pattern, they can change in terms of the quality of their formation. These changes manifest in the breaking up of the skin ridges themselves, causing them to take on a dotted appearance, sometimes referred to as "strings of pearls". Thus, whilst skin ridge patterns are indicative of congenital dispositions towards certain diseases, skin ridge quality can be indicative of disease conditions actually present. Skin ridge dissociation can only really be seen under a microscope or from a handprint as the detail of the skin ridges often cannot be clearly seen from the live hand itself.

Whilst skin ridge break-up has been recognised by medical dermatoglyphicists as a significant diagnostic phenomena only since the 1970s, the first investigations made into skin ridge dissociation were conducted by Noel Jaquin back in the 1930s. Jaquin found that skin ridge break-up is especially indicative of conditions of toxicity or inflammation, especially those brought about by bacterial infection. Jaquin noted that certain malformations of the ridges occurred in particular diseases, such as malaria, but also found that the ridges were very often dissociated in intestinal conditions and complaints. Interestingly, in modern times, skin ridge break-up has been noted by dermatoglyphicists to be common in both coeliac disease and intestinal obstruction, thus confirming Jaquin's original research.

Clear indications of Skin Ridge Dissociation

Following the discoveries of Noel Jaquin, the significance of skin ridge break-up itself varies according to the area of the palm on which it is found. The area of the hand where the skin ridge dissociation takes place is thought to be significant for ascertaining which organs of the body are affected.

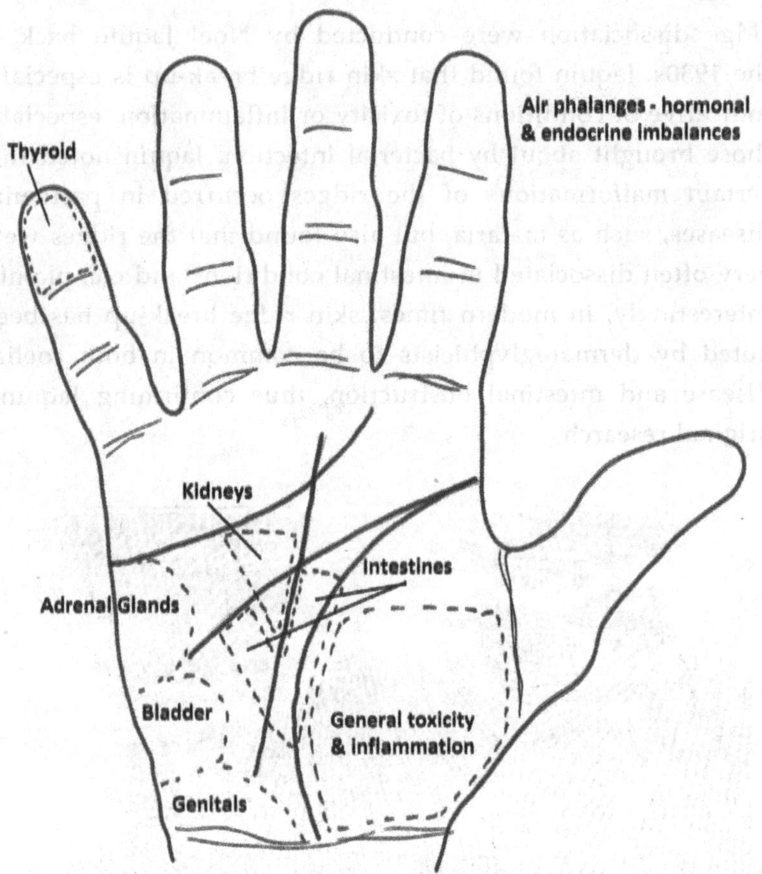

Skin Ridge Dissociation in the palm

General Toxicity – conditions of general toxicity of the body is shown by skin ridge break-up in the whole Earth quadrant. This could be caused by self-induced intoxication through the use of alcohol or drugs or could be indicative of general inflammatory conditions, bacterial infections or pre-cancerous conditions.

Intestinal Conditions – are shown by skin ridge break-up in the centre of the palm beneath the middle finger between the Major and Minor Earth line and beneath the ring finger between the Minor Earth and Major Air lines. This indicates some bacterial infection of the intestines or intestinal inflammation causing increased levels of toxicity.

Adrenal disturbances – are shown by break-up of the skin ridge patterns on the ulnar edge of the palm underneath the Water line.

Kidney disorders – are shown by the break-up of the skin ridges under the Ring finger between the Air and Water lines.

Bladder disorders – infections and inflammation affecting the bladder or the ureters or urethra are shown by skin ridge break-up in the mid Water Zone along the ulnar edge.

Gynaecological disorders – infections and inflammation of female pelvic organs are indicated by the break-up of the skin ridges in the lower Water Zone.

More on the Radial Loop on the Ring Finger

The Radial Loop on the Ring finger is extremely rare to find – which means it is quite difficult to develop a clear idea of its significance. However, this pattern is more commonly seen in the hands of those with Down Syndrome as we have noted. So, we have some clues to indicate what it is all about – people with Down Syndrome are generally exceptionally sociable and friendly.

Obviously, being found on the Ring finger this pattern will describe something of our social persona, how we relate to people, and our responsiveness to social groups. The socially responsive nature of those with Down Syndrome shows something of the social openness and warmth that this pattern might give. But I have also seen it in the hands of someone who is a Ronnie Wood look-a-like – the guitarist from the Rolling Stones – and who has been paid to impersonate him. It's like this pattern gives an ability to mimic – the ability to take on the persona of another person, such that one's social face (Ring finger) is derived from an external source (Radial Loop).

A recent study group with members of the International Hand Reading Association provided the opportunity to look into the significance of this pattern in more detail.[1] In one example, a woman described how, when she was a young girl, she was very intensely active, dynamic, hyper-active, assertive and almost aggressive. When she hit puberty, she suddenly became very self-conscious and changed her personality. Her "fiery" personality was no longer acceptable and as a result of her Radial Loop, she changed to be how other people wanted or expected her to be.

Others have suggested that this pattern gives an extraordinary sensitivity to others. It's not just empathy, but mental sensitivity that discerns the details of the other person's character, their needs and wants. A person with this ability can be described as being the perfect listener.

One example given was a veterinarian who is very understanding to her patients' owners. She is highly compassionate. She also has dealt with a lot of mental illness in her family and has exhibited extreme patience and understanding. She is very good at listening.

Another example is someone who works with children and is particularly good with autistic and special needs kids, knowing what they need and how to cope with them when others are at a loss. These children are particularly attracted to her and feel very safe and relaxed with her. She makes them feel secure.

The feeling that people with Radial Loops on the Ring finger generate is a feeling of acceptance, that they recognise you for yourself, and accept you for what you are, and will always honour the time they spend with you. When they are listening to you, it makes you feel like they know you really well, that you are the only person in the world. They are able to give you exactly what you need to hear at that moment.

One professional handreader I know can switch this ability on and off at will and brings this quality out when he is giving a consultation. He is a very good listener, naturally able to be fully present, fully there, observing and reflecting back. It shows the ability to fully give one's presence.

---

1. I am grateful to my colleagues in the International Hand Reading Association c2021 for discussions on this rare fingerprint pattern to elicit its meanings and signification. With especial thanks to Felicity Booth and Johnny Fincham.

Fingerprints of the Famous

There is one very rare fingerprint pattern that is very much a special case. It is a composite or compound pattern called a **Radial Peacock's Eye**. As we have seen, the (Ulnar) Peacock's Eye is most commonly seen on the Ring finger, occurring in around 11% of cases. However, a Peacock's Eye can also be found in a *Radial* Loop version. Since Radial Loops occur primarily on the Index finger, it is most likely that this is where a Radial Peacock's Eye is going to be found, if it is to be found at all. It is an extremely rare pattern, but one that nonetheless has special significance.[1]

Essentially, what we have here is a Whorl trapped inside a Radial Loop, so we see the qualities of both the Radial Loop and the Whorl going on. This is somebody who is both very strongly affected by the environment and who wants to retain a strong sense of their own individuality *at the same time*. They will be both easy going, moulding themselves to the people and circumstances around them in a relaxed manner – but also inevitably stamping their own original mark on it as well. They want to fit in *and* they want to stand out! Part of the way this pattern manifests is an oscillation between the tendencies of the one pattern followed by the inclinations of the other. For example, this could be a person who initially is very conformist when encountering a new group or situation, but then later has an intense urge to break free and start doing things their own way and on their terms. They have a love of freedom – but a fear of isolation.

Someone with a Radial Peacock's Eye on the Index finger will hate being boxed in, defined or trapped by the views of others. Yet, their success and individuality depend very much on the prevailing trends which they have so successfully copied. These are mimics who develop something that is very unique, giving an original twist to that which they have absorbed. They learn things very well and then add something to give it a flavour that is all their own. They are acutely aware of how others see them and how they are expected to behave yet will resist those influences. They will be a total maverick, unpredictable, constantly shape-shifting and changing their identity according to the needs of the Whorl or the Radial loop in alternation. This does not make for easy personal relationships. They will need to find a way to express the uniqueness of their personality, whilst at the same time, meet the approval of those around them.

A therapist with this pattern will be able to relate very openly to others but, rather than be washed away by the power of other people's emotions, will be able to maintain an independent sense of self-identity. Like deep-sea diving in a diving bell, the pattern suggests they have a kind of self-protection in other people's emotional oceans. Equally, in a social context, their personal philosophy of life will be the endeavour to express their individuality against the background noise of the social milieu. They will take something that many people do, and then do it in a completely new, innovative and ground-breaking way. They will see themselves as both someone who is breaking the mould but also someone who knows what that mould is, before they break it. They will feel good about themselves when they have come up with a new way of doing something that lifts the generally accepted *modus operandi*. These are true innovators who can connect what they are doing with the mood, vibe or general tone of what is already happening all around them. The Radial Loop means they can absorb all that and take all that on; the Whorl part of the pattern inspires them to make something different and original out of it.

Their life lessons are all about freedom and freedom of self-expression. They can be so torn between wanting to "be themselves" and wanting to fit in that their behaviour can appear erratic, one moment acquiescing to something and the next insisting on going their own way. As such, the Radial Peacock's Eye shows someone who oscillates between conformity and rebelliousness. They need a lot of time on their own to find the essence of who they are. Whilst they enjoy being in the company of others, solitude and time spent on their own is their ultimate solace.

The Fingerprints of Jimi Hendrix

Jimi Hendrix is one of the most iconic figures of popular culture from the 1960s. From his flamboyant dress sense to his laid-back manner, he became the "poster-boy" for the 1960s counter-culture movement, from Haight-Ashbury in 1967 to Woodstock in 1969. In Jimi Hendrix we see the *zeitgeist* of the hippy, flower-power, counter-cultural revolution, someone who still stands as an iconic representation of those times even today.

Obviously, Hendrix was a phenomenal guitarist, innovating a guitar style that is still being emulated by young aspiring guitar players. One thing that is clear from the photos of his hands is that he had very large hands which some argue contributed to his unique playing style. But what other features of his hands might show that? Unfortunately, nearly all the extant photos of Hendrix show his hands playing or holding his guitar and I have not yet seen an image of his palm and palmar lines. However, we do have a copy of his police records from when he was arrested in Canada in May 1966 for possession of narcotics, so we do know what his fingerprints were.[2]

Jimi Hendrix's Fingerprints

Right hand (passive): Whorl – Radial Loop – Loop – Whorl – Loop

Left hand (active): Double loop – **Radial Peacock's Eye** – Loop – Loop – Loop

In summary: two whorls, two radial loops, one double loop and five loops.

It is as important to remember that whilst Hendrix played the guitar with his left hand, he was actually ambidextrous. The fingerprints on both hands are therefore significant.

The five Loop fingerprints make Hendrix a congenial and sociable kind of guy, but despite their numerical dominance, they are not the most important fingerprints in his hand. The most obvious fingerprint that one would expect to see in Hendrix's hands is a **Whorl on the Ring finger**. The Ring finger is all about appearance, performance, creativity and artistic expression and someone with a Whorl on this finger has an unusual and interesting personal aesthetic. Which is to say, they have their own unique style, flair and fashion sense and seek to express their individuality through their appearance and the way that they present themselves. Whorls on ring fingers are, of course, also commonly found in the hands of artists, musicians and performers.

Hendrix also has a **Whorl on his Thumb** which shows a strong-minded individual who likes to do his own thing on his own terms and in his own way. Whorls here give a strong need for freedom, independence and autonomy, a desire to not be restricted by others in his choices and decision making.

However, he has a **Double Loop pattern on his left Thumb** which indicates that he can be more conciliatory in direct interactions with other people. He is good at resolving conflict between people as he can see both sides to any situation. Double Loops are often good at synthesis, bringing together disparate people, or in this case, disparate sound styles – and integrating them. On a personal level, he would have been known as someone who changed his plans, almost indecisively; but he would likely argue that he was going with the flow and being accommodating to the arising changes in circumstances. Sometimes described as a *Loop of Fluctuance*, the Double Loop fingerprint pattern on the Thumb gives a fluid and adaptable response to the world. Though, underneath all of that, the need for autonomy and freedom as shown by the Whorl on the right-hand Thumb will prevail.

On his right hand, he has a **Radial Loop on his Index finger** which shows that his sense of self-identity is dependent upon and strongly influenced by the people and circumstances around him. Because the loop opens from the Thumb side of the hand, he is very influenced by external factors, and hence his sense of who he is changes according to whom he is with. If we look at photographs of him playing guitar with the Isley Brothers or with Little Richard, we see a very different Hendrix than the one we are accustomed to from the Woodstock posters. With a Radial Loop on his Index finger, he has developed a life-strategy to not only adapt to the people and situations around him, but also to *adopt* the attitudes and values of those around him. The pattern shows something of a chameleon-like ability to take on board the shape and colour of the people, situations and circumstances around him and *become* that.

> [H]e was a visionary who collapsed the genre boundaries of rock, soul, blues, and jazz and an iconic figure whose appeal linked the concerns of white hippies and black revolutionaries by clothing black anger in the colourful costumes of London's Carnaby Street.
>
> Charles Shaar Murray[3]

Those with Radial Loop fingerprint patterns merge, blend and absorb, moulding themselves to the influences around them – clearly something that Hendrix did in his musical approach. He not only took on different approaches to music, they became his *identity*. People with Radial Loop fingerprints on their Index finger can quite easily lose themselves in the values, influences and cultural impressions of things that are going on around them.

But what is especially interesting is that the fingerprint on his active hand Index finger is a **Radial Peacock's Eye**. This rare fingerprint variant is a Radial Loop fingerprint pattern, but with a whorl in the centre of it! So, there is an interesting combination here of taking on board that which he found in the environment around him *and* making it highly individual and distinctive at the same time. The whorl, being the mark of the individualist, shows that whilst he was strongly influenced by the mood and vibes of his day, he would also stamp his own distinctive mark upon it.

In Hendrix's case, he took on the entire late 1960's *zeitgeist* and in a way is still carrying that burden today. He would have craved time and space by himself, outside the company of all others, so he could be free of other people's expectations of him. He would have wanted to create some space in his life where he could be alone with himself and his guitar and not "be" what other people wanted him to be. All that fame and being in the spotlight would have been a burden for this otherwise shy and sensitive guy.

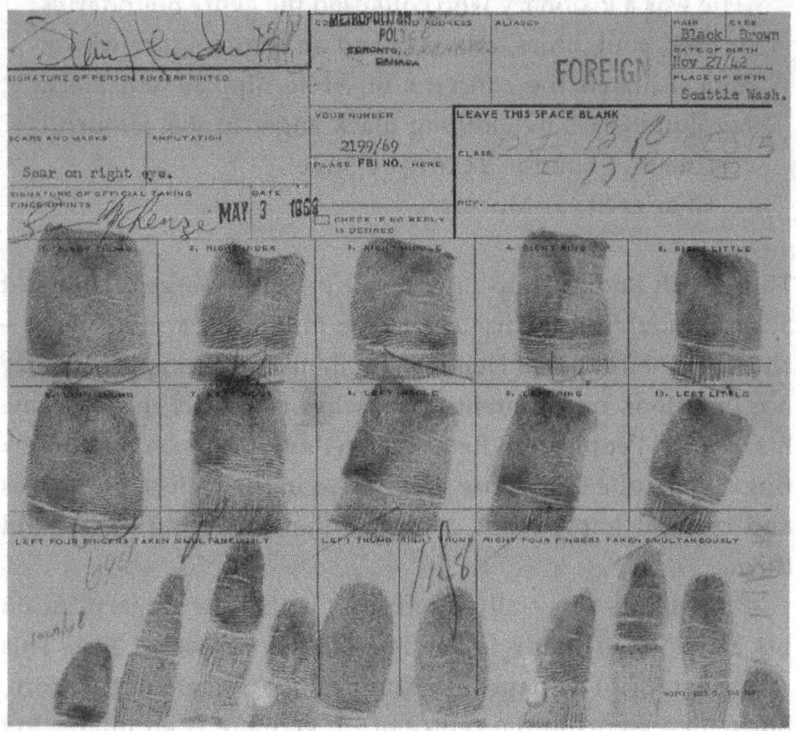

SIGNATURE OF PERSON FINGERPRINTED
METROPOLITAN POLICE
TORONTO,
CANADA
ALIASES
FOREIGN
HAIR Black
EYES Brown
DATE OF BIRTH Nov 27/42
PLACE OF BIRTH Seattle Wash.
YOUR NUMBER 2199/69
PLACE FBI NO. HERE
LEAVE THIS SPACE BLANK
CLASS
REF.
SCARS AND MARKS
AMPUTATION
Scar on right eye.
SIGNATURE OF OFFICIAL TAKING FINGERPRINTS
DATE MAY 3 1969
CHECK IF NO REPLY IS DESIRED
10. LEFT LITTLE
LEFT FOUR FINGERS TAKEN SIMULTANEOUSLY
LEFT THUMB
RIGHT THUMB
RIGHT FOUR FINGERS TAKEN SIMULTANEOUSLY

The fingerprints of Jimi Hendrix

The Fingerprints of John Lennon

> My role in society, or any artist's or poet's role, is to try and express what we all feel. Not to tell people how to feel. Not as a preacher, not as a leader, but as a reflection of us all.
>
> John Lennon

John Lennon (1940–1980) was one of the founding members of and the guitarist, singer and songwriter for The Beatles, perhaps the most musically influential band of all time. Born in Liverpool, UK, he eventually moved to live in the USA where he died in 1980 when he was assassinated. From immigration records, his fingerprints were taken for his application for permanent residency in the USA in July 1976 and we can see that he had:

Right Hand: Loop – Radial Loop – Whorl – Whorl – Loop
Left Hand: Loop – Whorl – Whorl – Whorl – Loop

In summary, Lennon has five Whorls, four Ulnar Loops, and one Radial Loop. Of these, the Whorls and the Radial Loop are most important from a psychological point of view.

John Lennon

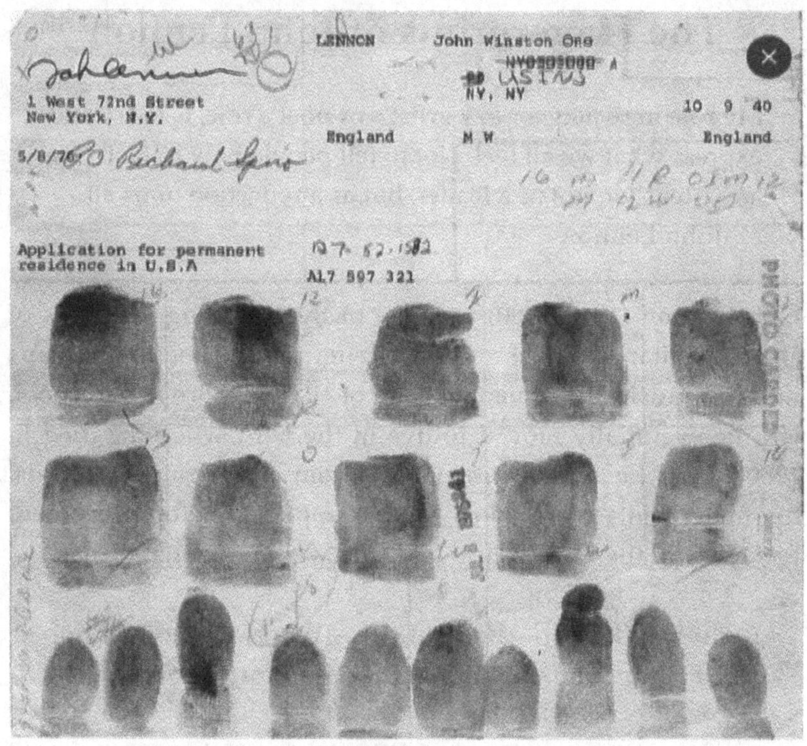

The Fingerprints of John Lennon[4]

Whorl Dominant Hand

With five Whorls on his hands, what we have here is someone who is a rebel, a radical and an individualist. This is somebody who does not want to have a conventional life and wants to go his own way, travel a road in life that has not been travelled before. People with multiple Whorls (especially five or more) are innovators, people who challenge the status quo and want to effect change in the world. They stand apart from their contemporaries and are bold enough to go off and do their own thing, regardless of what other people think of them. Integrity, independence and autonomy are essential for them, they are self-motivated and often highly talented. They can be principled and have difficulty compromising with others over issues that are important to them. Frequently, they feel different from other people and this can cause them to be something of a loner. The Whorl on his Index finger (left hand) shows that he wants to be his own boss and wants to live life on his own terms, according to his own personal philosophies and values. This is someone who thinks for himself and does not tolerate interference from others and will actively rebel if he feels restricted or hampered in any way. Having lots of Whorls can lead to a feeling of being misunderstood by others or a feeling that he does not really belong, a sense of being a social outcast or misfit. His need to express his individuality and to have the freedom to do so may at times have come across as arrogance.

Radial Loop on the Water Finger

Having said that, the fingerprint on the Index finger of his right hand is a **Radial Loop**, showing that this is someone who is thoughtful and reflective but also someone who is somewhat reactive to the world around him. This fingerprint pattern can show a psychological defensiveness which Lennon manifested through his ability to invoke scathing sarcasm. The Radial Loop also gives something of a chameleonic characteristic, reflected in the many changes in appearance that he went through over the years. In particular, this pattern can show a lack of self-worth and a need for approval or affection from others and is often seen in the hands of people who felt criticised or rejected by a parent when young. His defensiveness is therefore a vulnerability protection mechanism. As he is strongly influenced by people, he is careful who he allows to get close to him, which in the first instance was Paul McCartney and then later Yoko Ono. Her arrival would direct his primary allegiance to her, as can be seen in the later Beatles film footage. Whilst he might see and feel his relationship with her as a melding or merging, others might see that he has become overcome with or subsumed by the person that he has allowed into his life.

There is a suggestion of a ridge re-curvature in the centre of this Radial Loop which, although not as pronounced as the example in the hand of Jimi Hendrix, suggests that Lennon also had a Radial Peacock's Eye pattern. This fingerprint gives a combination of both being responsive to prevailing social trends and musical influences but also being someone who wants to put their own take on it. As we saw with Hendrix, there is an interesting combination here of taking on board that which is in the cultural milieu *and* making it highly individual and distinctive at the same time, of being strongly influenced by the *zeitgeist*, but at the same time putting their own distinctive mark upon it. It is almost extraordinary to consider that two of the most iconic figures of 1960s counter-culture both had the same extraordinarily unusual fingerprint on their Index fingers!

Music, Acting and Performance

As a performing musician, we should fully expect to see Whorls on both Lennon's Ring fingers, especially as his Ring fingers are long in both hands. Long Ring fingers are extremely common in musicians, actors, artists and performers and having a Whorl on this finger adds originality and creativity. It gives an interest in self-expression, colour, aesthetics – and colourful clothing! Anything that allows him artistic or creative outlet is of interest. These features show that Lennon was a natural performer and entertainer with a love of having fun and joking around. People with long Ring fingers are sociable and gregarious and often seek attention or approbation from others. However, being in a band would have been challenging for Lennon – because he naturally prefers to work by himself. Having so many Whorls, he would prefer to be his own boss so that he has control and autonomy over what he was doing. This may have been a factor in why The Beatles split up, particularly after their manager, Brian Epstein, died and McCartney visibly took the lead in the band as Lennon withdrew into his heroin experimentation with Yoko Ono.

The pronounced lower joint of his thumb shows a strong sense of timing and it is notable that his main musical role in the band was as the rhythm guitarist. The long Ring finger shows that he would have loved the fun of musical performance and the drama and excitement that went with being a Beatle. Long Ring fingers are also found in the hands of actors and in addition to The Beatles' movies, Lennon also had a significant part in the anti-war movie *How I won the War* (1966). The top phalange of his thumb is visibly pliable, a characteristic feature often seen in the hands of actors.

Whorls on the Earth Fingers

Given that Whorls are more likely to be found firstly on Ring (Fire) fingers and secondly on Index (Water) fingers, of particular note then are the *homologous Whorls* on the Middle (Earth) fingers. The presence of a Whorl on these fingers indicates a thoughtful and analytical disposition; he is quick thinking and grasps idea quickly. It shows he has clearly formed opinions about things and can be rather argumentative and it's very hard to get him to change his mind or to persuade him to think otherwise. Many Whorled people can be very difficult to get along with. They are very much a law unto themselves and often have an inward disregard of others and the society in which they live. They are only adaptable if they want to be, and being much less tied by convention, they are only conventional and law-abiding as long as it suits them to be so. The more Whorls on the hand, the more the individual will reject society and any imposition of values that they don't agree with.

John Lennon and Yoko Ono's "Bed Peace" protest, 1969

Specifically, Whorls on the middle finger show someone who questions and challenges the political and philosophical values of the culture into which they are born. In 1965, Lennon was awarded the MBE by the Queen but returned it four years later as an anti-war protest. Consequently, Lennon is perhaps known as much for the political stances that he took in his life as he was for his music, particularly with regard to his protests to end the war in Vietnam.

Imagine that.

For all we are saying, is give peace a chance.

The Fingerprints of Malcolm X

Malcom X was a prominent black human rights activist in the civil rights movement of the 1960s in the USA who was assassinated in 1965. He has some very unusual fingerprints, including *two* Radial Nutant Loops.

Malcolm X

Right Hand: Radial Nutant Loop – Arch – Arch – Whorl – Loop
Left Hand: Arch – Radial Nutant Loop – Loop – Loop – Loop

The middle finger of the right hand has one recurving ridge, so technically this can be classed as a Loop. But it is so low-lying that its effects will come out as an Arch. In effect, Malcolm X has three Arch patterns, so this is an Arch dominant hand. Arches on the middle fingers are very concerned with social justice, fairness before the law and the application of just and rightful law. The Arch is fairly rare on the middle finger unless found with Arches on other digits. This pattern can be seen in the hands of lawyers, criminologists, anthropologists and social workers.

The Whorl needs to be considered as unusual in this hand as there is an inverse relationship between Whorls and

Arches in the hand and one does not usually find a hand with both these prints together. In Malcolm X's case, given the extreme length of his Ring finger, this gives him strong presentational and promotional skills. He is concerned with getting a message across to people and will be concerned to present himself in a way that is appealing and acceptable. Men with long Ring fingers with Whorls on them are usually well presented and distinctively dressed, as Malcolm X always was.

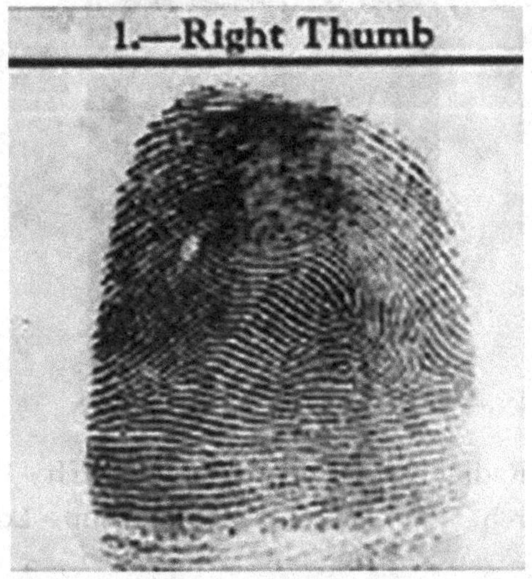

Nutant Radial Loop

The most significant and unusual pattern is the **Radial Nutant Loop**, which is an extremely rare fingerprint pattern. Sometimes it is considered to be a horizontal Radial Loop, which is a fair description; but it is classed as a Nutant Loop and described as such by Cherrill (1954), though he does not give any indication of its frequency except that it seems to be very rare. Scotland Yard statistics show that Composites are found in 0.162% of fingerprints and Accidentals in only 0.046% of fingerprints – and Nutant Loops are rarer than this!

From an interpretative point of view, it can be classed as a Radial Loop Having such a pattern on the thumb would show someone who was very sensitive to and responsive to the "will of the people".

This is someone who can sense the mood of the moment and move with the zeitgeist and be a spokesperson for that – as with Jimi Hendrix. But with the radial loop also on the thumb, this is more to do with will, power and political control and the effect of personal action on the collective, all of which are provenances of the thumb.

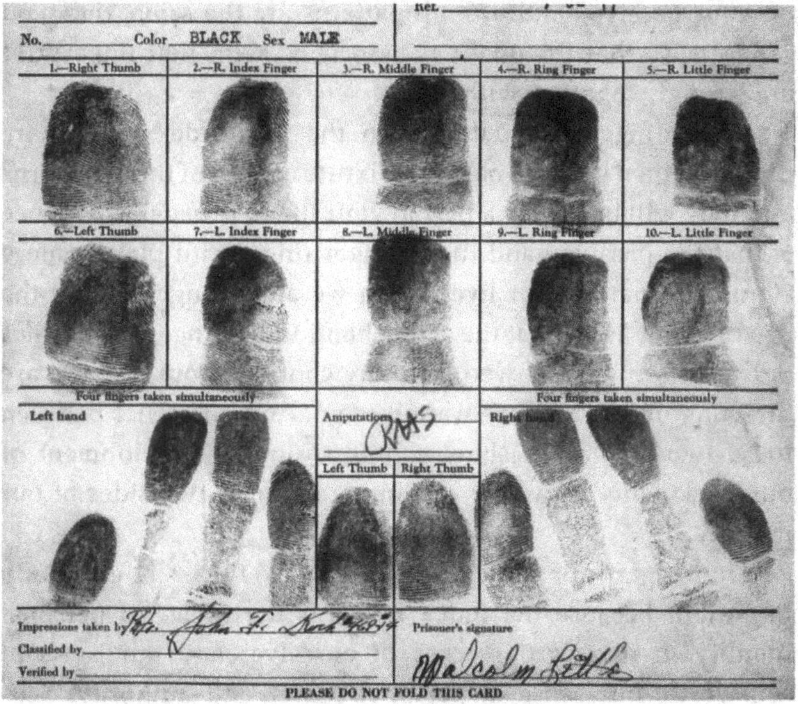

The Fingerprints of Malcolm X[5]

---

1. **C Abrams *Radial Loops and Whorls* Journal of the Cheirological Society v349/2 1998**
2. **Courtesy of AJ Washington http://www.dermatoglyphics. com/**
3. **Charles Shaar Murray https://www.britannica.com/ biography/Jimi-Hendrix**
4. **Courtesy of AJ Washington http://www.dermatoglyphics. com/**
5. **Courtesy of AJ Washington http://www.dermatoglyphics. com/**

Fingerprints and Your Personal Identity

When looking at your own hands, the best way to start to decipher the significance of your fingerprints is to consider the fingerprint to be found on your Index finger. Once you have correctly identified which type of fingerprint you have on your active hand (the right hand in right-handed people, the left hand in left-handed people), have a look also at the Index finger on your passive hand. If both patterns are the same, then you can be sure that the qualities associated with that fingerprint are strongly manifest within you.

If the fingerprint patterns on the two Index fingers are different, then you will be an admixture of both of those patterns and they will both play a part in your life. The usual experience is that the passive hand Index finger fingerprint plays a more significant part in our lives when we are younger (under the age of about 24) whilst the active hand Index fingerprint comes out more strongly as we take more control of our life and are directing life the way we want it to go. Any difference between these two prints can show a progression or development of our personality as we try and integrate these two sides of our identity.

The fingerprint pattern on the Index finger is especially important because the Index finger is the finger of personal identity. It reveals our sense of ourselves and our sense of self-worth, our sense of personal power and authority. Self-confidence and self-belief are shown by the condition of this finger as are issues of self-worth and self-doubt. Moreover, given that the Index finger is ruled by the element Water, it is an indicator of how a person *feels* about themselves, it shows something of our *felt-sense* of who we are. It is a reflection of our self-image and self-esteem, how you think of yourself and how you see yourself. It reveals something of your self-understanding and self-awareness as well as being an indicator of your personal values, ideals and aspirations and your goals in life. It is a digital expression of who you are and your personal philosophy of life.

The statements below have been collected from people with these particular fingerprint patterns on their Index fingers.[1]

Arch

I see myself as someone who is down to earth and practical.

I see myself as someone who is reliable, independent, supportive and resilient.

I feel good about myself when I am able to support, nurture and help other people.

I like being useful and of service to others.

I enjoy making things.

My confidence is augmented when I am appreciated for being helpful.

I feel good when I feel secure.

I feel good about myself when I help people and when I make things.

I take my responsibilities seriously and don't do things by halves.

I hate it when I take on too much responsibility (which I tend to do).

I hate it when I am being rushed or have to respond spontaneously.

I don't like it when I don't know how I can be of help.

I need certainty and stability.

My family is important to me.

I need a secure base to rise from and a few close friends/ family.

Ulnar Loop

I see myself as someone who is flexible and adaptable.

I am easy going.

I get on well with others.

People are important to me.

I feel good about myself when I have a sense of connection with others.

My friendships are important to me.

I like joining in, being part of a team, having a sense of community.

My confidence is augmented when I have positive feelings about myself.

Having a sense of being connected with others feels good.

I hate it when people are left out.

I don't like being left on my own.

I need friendship and camaraderie.

Radial Loop

I see myself as someone who adapts easily to others, is flexible, easy going, friendly, responsive, and adaptable. However, I can easily be overwhelmed.

I feel good about myself when helping other people.

I feel good about myself when other people give me positive feedback.

I like reflecting things back to other people.

I am good at empathic listening.

My leadership style is one of consensus.

I am good at listening and sensing what is needed and then can provide that.

I feel good about myself when I understand my environment and can adapt to it as needed.

I feel good when I know what is expected of me.

My confidence is augmented when I am praised and when I receive positive feedback from others.

I hate it when others are critical of me and when I feel "not good enough".

I don't like getting things wrong.

I don't like being criticised. I like being praised.

My confidence is augmented when I get words of support from people that are close to me.

I hate it when I am being criticized.

I need some time alone even though most of the time I like to have a few good friends around.

I need space to find myself again after spending time with others.

I need lots of alone time to hear my inner voice.

I often compare myself to others and feel "less than".

I am very sensitive to judgement, criticism and negative feedback.

I feel good about myself when I have plenty of time and space to myself to be me.

I feel good about myself when I am working on self-discovery and when I am in a nurturing environment where I am encouraged.

My confidence is augmented when I am praised.

I hate it when I am criticised.

I hate it when I spend too much time with other people and feel I am losing myself.

I need space.

I like spending time alone or with people who understand me.

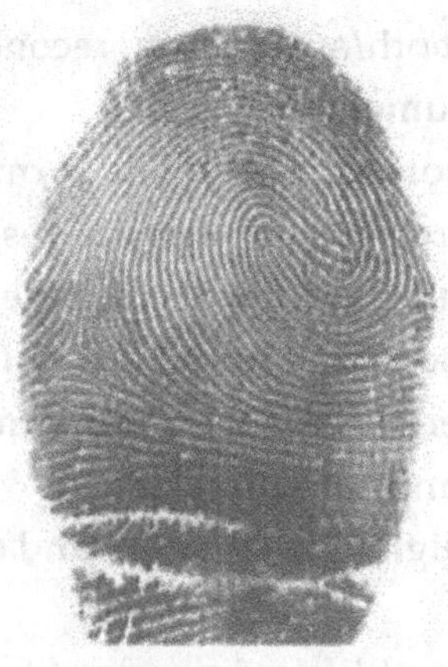

Double Loop

I am someone who has lots of doubt.

I vacillate between options.

My feelings can fluctuate quite wildly from confidence to self-doubt, ups and down, turmoil.

I am often uncertain.

I can feel confused or unclear.

I am someone who has changeable feelings about my intimate relationships.

I can feel unsure.

I see myself as someone who has struggled with self-doubt most of my life and have often been confused about who I am and why I am here.

I can be indecisive.

I hate making decisions.

My confidence is augmented when I don't allow doubt to prevail.

I hate it when I have to make a decision.

I see myself as someone who is indecisive.

I see myself as a both/and person, reconciling options, seeing both sides of an argument.

I see myself as someone who is a formidable mediator as I apprehend and appreciate all perspectives.

I feel good about myself when I have worked out how to balance various options and found a way forward.

I like it when there is balance and harmony.

I hate it when things are not clear.

I need time to weigh up a situation and evaluate the best way to proceed.

The spiritual side of life is important to me.

Tented Arch

I see myself as someone who is full of energy and enthusiasm.

I like there being noise and activity around me.

I feel good about myself when I am on my mission and fulfilling my dreams.

I like taking the initiative and leading others.

I like to inspire and motivate people

My confidence is augmented when I am able to inspire others.

I hate it when I have nothing to do and things are quiet.

I need a project, a dream to pursue, an ideal to attain and people to activate.

I need good people around me to lift and inspire me.

Whorl

I see myself as someone who is independent, going my own way.

I see myself as someone who is a bit different.

I want to be accepted for being different.

I am true to myself, creative and original.

I feel good about myself when I can freely express myself with integrity.

I like being independent, free to do things my way in my own time.

I like being on my own. I need to have lots of time and space alone.

I like being independent and taking risks, such as travelling alone.

I hate it when I am pressured to behave or do something which doesn't feel true to me.

I feel good about myself when I am on my own.

I like being different and don't fit easily into groups.

I like having my own space.

I like to think for myself.

My confidence is augmented when I can act autonomously and am left to do it my way.

My confidence is enhanced when I speak and act from integrity.

My confidence is augmented when I am free to do things my own way and in my own time.

I hate it when people tell me what to do or when I am constrained by the demands of others.

I need space and freedom to be me.

I can't give the best unless I've got room to move.

---

1. **With especial thanks to the Auckland Chirological Study group 2023 for their contributions**

Fingerprints and Your Karmic Path

Each of the different fingerprint patterns describe different motivational forces that give emphases in people's lives about what they think is important. The dominant fingerprint pattern to be found in the hand will show a person's priorities, needs, goals and ambitions. The dominant pattern will also show specific challenges and difficulties they may encounter as well. What is evident from looking at hands for forty years is that the experiences of people's lives play out according to the significant fingerprint patterns that they have within their hands. And it becomes obvious that their lives have been very strongly shaped by these forces. Which is to say, also, if you know what kinds of fingerprint patterns you have, you can know the kinds of things that are more likely to happen to you, whether that be due to a genetic disposition towards certain diseases or due to a particular skill or talent that you were born with from which you have forged your career.

The hand is a map of karma and the life-lessons, lessons for us in this lifetime, can be seen by assessing the balance of fingerprint pattern types to be found on the ends of our fingers. In addition to looking at the fingerprint pattern to be found on your Index finger, also assess which fingerprint pattern is *dominant* in your hand, out of ten.

Eight or more Ulnar loops means you are a Loop dominant person.

Five or more Whorls means you are a Whorl dominant person.

Three or more Arches means you are an Arch dominant person.

With regard to the Minor Dermatoglyphics, even just having one of these can be enough for an over-riding effect of that pattern within that person's life, especially if it is a Radial

Loop fingerprint pattern. But, as we have seen, all of the minor dermatoglyphics are more common on the Index finger in any case, so the dermatoglyphic on the Index finger is especially significant precisely because this finger expresses our self-identity, our personal psychology and our spiritual ideals and aspirations.

Ulnar Loops (Water) (8+)

With an abundance of Ulnar Loops, you play a vital role in bringing people together. Your purpose is to promote co-operation and inclusion, to ensure no one is left out or left behind. You show the world how to live with flexibility and compromise as you seek to promote harmony in human social and emotional interaction. Your life lessons are around individuality in relation to group identity, and acceptance.

Arches (Earth) (3+)

The role of those with Arches is to provide support, ensuring that people feel safe and have "enough". Your life revolves around nurturing others, providing security and creating a foundation for others to flourish, like plants thriving in fertile soil. You give strength by being a container, being able to hold space for others. You need and create security, stability – and family. Your life lessons are around trust, fidelity and loyalty.

Tented Arches (Fire) (1+)

Your life task is to inspire and ignite, to enthuse others and illuminate the path to new possibilities. By taking risks and going in new directions, your initiative provides leadership. Your life lessons are about finding meaning and purpose in your life – you need to find your mission!

Whorls (Air) (5+)

If you have Whorls, your mission in life is to free yourself from the shackles of convention, to be a change-maker, to break the rules, to innovate, to find new ways of doing things. Show others how to be fearless in your individuality and apply that for the greater good. Be original and live differently. Your life lessons are around finding your unique place in the world and balancing the individual need for autonomy and independence with that of being in service to the greater good.

Double Loops (Water) (2+)

Your life challenge is to rise above the confusion of duality to be the broker of peace, offering reconciliation in situations where there is dispute as you see both sides. Become the arbitrator and seek unity where there is conflict; create harmony where there is discord. You are a born negotiator. Your life lessons are around reconciling differences and apparent opposites, and the integration of the spiritual and the mundane.

Radial Loop (Water) (1+)

The life path here is to seek acceptance of yourself and others, to release the fear of judgement. Open up, be sensitive and receptive to others yet lose concern over what other people think. Your self-worth is not dependent on the opinions of others. Learn to be on your own and find stillness within so as to be a positive reflection of the best qualities of others. Your life lessons are around maintaining your responsiveness to others without being subsumed or overwhelmed by them, developing the ability to maintain your own personal boundaries by finding the quiet space within.

* * *

Of course, we now know that not only do the fingerprints describe something of our unique personality, because of their unchanging nature, they describe something of our personal identity over time. They are constant biometric markers of the way consciousness is interacting with the phenomenal world through our physical being, a pattern of expression that stays the same for at least this lifetime. But whilst the fingerprints are unchanging genetic and karmic markers, it is the lines of the hands that describe our present experience and our present patterns of suffering. It is, therefore, comforting to know that the lines of the hands change over time as a reflection of our personal evolution and, especially, in response to changing patterns of stress, health and wellness.

If you change how you experience your life, then the lines of the hands will change accordingly.

Your life is literally in your hands.

About the Author

Christopher Jones has been a leading figure in the world of handreading for over 40 years and was the Secretary of the UK Cheirological Society from 1989–1999 writing for and publishing their quarterly *Journal of Studies*. During that time, he taught many handreaders who went on to become expert chirologists in their respective countries, including Israel, Spain, Croatia, Australia, Sweden, South Africa, Canada and the UK. The written works of his students are amongst the most esteemed books on handreading available today.

The author of fifteen technical study books on chirology, Christopher wrote a definitive guide to the History of Handreading after five years of study in the libraries of Oxford University. He has conducted original chirological research into health assessment from the hand, the effects of meditation on the hand, the hands of criminals and the hands of drug addicts and facilitated advanced chirological study seminars with noted handreaders such as Johnny Fincham, Felicity Booth, Lynn Seal, Johan Hjelmborg, Talma Brill, Laura Thornton and Chris Swain. Whilst at Oxford, he completed a Master's degree in Philosophy and Theology and ran the Oxford Astrology Group with Dr Charlotte Suthrell, combining psychological astrology with traditional horary astrology.

Christopher first took Refuge as a Buddhist in 1983 and his training in esoteric Buddhism is infused into the practice of handreading to provide a thorough, erudite and enlightening perspective on how to live with integrity and authenticity.

Note to Reader

If you are interested in learning more about this approach to handreading you will find a number of resources available online which I have established. In addition to my offerings on social media, my website and YouTube channel provide interesting articles and video presentations which outline the scope and range of subjects covered in modern chirology, so this is a good place to start. For more serious students of handreading, there is also my Patreon site which has been set up for students who are actively studying chirology. You will find links to courses that I teach amongst these pages.

Facebook: www.facebook.com/handreadingnz
Instagram: www.instagram.com/handreadingnz
You Tube: www.youtube.com/@MasterHandreader
Website: www.handreading.nz
Patreon: www.patreon.com/handreading

Studying Chirological Handreading

If you are interested in studying handreading to a professional level, then you are invited to contact me to enquire about the courses that I run. Whilst these are taught in person for people living in New Zealand, these courses are also available online in different formats – Zoom classes over three months, Six-month Immersion for Personal Tuition and in self-study video format.

Students who graduate from these classes are invited to become a member of the International Hand Reading Association, an international professional organisation for practising handreaders. Membership is by subscription. The IHRA organises annual handreading conferences and encourages and supports all handreaders who have an ethical and compassionate approach to handreading. Several IHRA tutors run print reading classes on a regular and ongoing basis, as well as teaching courses on the principles and practice of chirological hand analysis.

International Hand Reading Association (IHRA)

For professional development
Ethical Handreading
Tuition and Mentoring
International Handreading Conferences
Founding Committee: Christopher Jones, Johnny Fincham, Felicity Booth, Lynn Seal
www.handreadinginternational.com

Appendix One: Fingerprint Distributions

Here is the statistical breakdown of the distribution of the different fingerprint pattern types on each of the digits. Based on my own study (Oxford 1991), I have divided the dermatoglyphic distribution into four categories based on how frequently they occurred on each digit. More than about 20% occurrence is classed as Common; between 5% and 15% is classed as Occasional. Less than 5% occurrence makes the pattern Uncommon, whereas less than 2% makes the pattern Rare.

For comparative purposes, I have also included the results of the surveys conducted by Scotland Yard in 1905 (n=5,000) and 1954 (n=10,000)[1] and a more recent survey of fingerprints collected by New Scotland Yard from 1977 (n=2,000,000).[2] The Oxford 1991 and 1905 Scotland Yard statistics did not differentiate gender or distributions on the right or left hands. It can be supposed that Scotland Yard will have taken more fingerprints of men; my sample would have contained more women than men as more women come for hand readings than men, which may account for some of the variations in our findings.

The 1954 Scotland Yard survey also did not differentiate gender but did consider right and left hands separately. I have averaged those together for the purposes of this tabulation for ease of comparison, as I have done also for the New Scotland Yard sample. The Caucasian distribution from New Scotland Yard 1977 has been kept as separated figures for males and females to reflect gender differences in fingerprint distributions. Note that the Peacock's Eye/Compound pattern was not differentiated in that survey so no comparative figures can be given for that fingerprint.

Common Patterns

Digit & Dermatoglyphic	Oxford	Scotland Yard		New Scotland Yard	
	1991	1905	1954	M 1977	F
Ulnar Loop on Little finger	80.2%	87.6	85%	85.1%	86.5%
Ulnar Loop on Middle finger	66%	74.1	71%	70%	71.4%
Ulnar Loop on the Thumb	62%	60.9	62%	62.3%	64.2%
Ulnar Loop on the Ring finger	51.4%	62.3	56.5%	55.9%	59.8%
Whorl on the Ring finger	30.8%	28.5	34.5%	38.5%	34.1%
Ulnar Loop on the Index finger	30.2%	35.2	33%	31.3%	34.6%
Whorl on the Index finger	25.2%	23.5	21.5%	24.4%	24.7%
Radial Loop on Index finger	20.4%	24.7	24%	22.8%	17.9%
Whorl on the Thumb	19.4%	25.5	18.5%	20.2%	17.5%

Here we can clearly see that the Ulnar Loop is the most common pattern on *all* digits – and for four of the digits, by a very large margin – and it is least common on the Index finger.

As a result, the pattern on the Index finger is almost equally divided between the Ulnar Loop, the Whorl and the Radial Loop.

The Index finger is the only digit on which the Radial Loop pattern is common.

The most common place to find a Whorl is on the Ring finger, but they are also common on the Index finger and the Thumb.

Occasional Patterns

Digit & Dermatoglyphic	Oxford	Scotland Yard		New Scotland Yard	
	1991	1905	1954	M 1977	F
Arch on the Index finger	13.6%	8.5%	7%	7.4%	10.4%
Arch on the Middle finger	13.0%	6.3%	5.5%	6.4%	8.7%
Whorl on the Middle finger	12.6%	13.5%	14.5%	15.6%	12.8%
Double Loop on the Thumb	11.2%	9.3%	15.5%	14.3%	12.6%
Peacock's Eye on Ring finger	10.8%	5.1%	2.5%	n/a	n/a
Whorl on the Little finger	10.6%	9.1%	10%	11.7%	9.6%
Arch on the Thumb	6.2%	3.5%	3.5%	2.9%	5.3%

As we can see, the Arch pattern is most frequently found on the Index and Middle fingers.

The Double Loop is most common on the Thumb.

The Peacock's Eye occurs most frequently on the Ring finger, even in the Scotland Yard statistics.

The Whorl is least common on the Little finger.

Uncommon Patterns

Digit & Dermatoglyphic	Oxford	Scotland Yard		New Scotland Yard	
	1991	1905	1954	M 1977	F
Peacock's Eye on Little finger	4.6%	1.8%	0.65%	n/a	n/a
Double Loop on Index finger	4.4%	0.5%	6.8%	1.6%	0.8%
Arch on the Ring finger	4.4%	2.3%	1.75%	1.9%	3.1%
Tented Arch on Index finger	4.0%	2.1%	2%	6.8%	6.3%
Double Loop on Middle finger	3.8%	1.7%	3.5%	2.9%	2.2%
Arch on the Little finger	3.4%	0.8%	0.9%	1.1%	2.3%
Radial Loop on Middle finger	2.4%	2.5%	3%	2.3%	1.8%

The most uncommon of the minor dermatoglyphs, the Tented Arch, occurs most frequently on the Index finger.

The Arch is least common on the Little finger.

Rare Patterns

Digit & Dermatoglyphic	Oxford	Scotland Yard		New Scotland Yard	
	1991	1905	1954	M 1977	F
Peacock's Eye on Index finger	1.2%	2.2%	1.9%	n/a	n/a
Peacock's Eye Middle finger	1.2%	1.0%	0.67%	n/a	n/a
Double Loop on Little finger	1.0%	0.5%	2.1%	1.6%	1.1%
Peacock's Eye on Thumb	0.8%	0.5%	0.17%	n/a	n/a
Tented Arch on Middle finger	0.8%	0.7%	0.53%	2.6%	2.9%
Radial Loop on Ring finger	0.8%	1.0%	0.88%	0.9%	1.0%
Double Loop on Ring finger	0.8%	0.9%	2.62%	2.2%	1.3%
Radial Loop on the Thumb	0.6%	0.2%	0.25%	0.2%	0.3%
Tented Arch on Ring finger	0.4%	0.1%	0.19%	0.4%	0.7%
Radial Loop on Little finger	0%	0.1%	0.11%	0.2%	0.2%
Tented Arch on Little finger	0%	0.01%	0.025%	0.3%	0.6%
Tented Arch on the Thumb	0%	0.01%	0%	0.01%	0.01%

The Radial Loop is extremely rare on the Thumb and Ring finger and almost never seen on the Little finger.

However, the Tented Arch clearly shows itself to be the rarest of all the dermatoglyphic patterns, on all digits. Even on the Index finger where it is most frequently found, its average occurrence is only 4.2%.

Full Set of Fingerprints

Aside from Ulnar Loops, to have a predominance of one type of print is not common:

Seven or more Ulnar Loops (45.6%) – about 1 in 2 people have seven or more Loops
Seven or more Whorls (10%) – about 1 in 10 people have seven or more Whorls
Seven or more Arches (2.8%) – about 1 in 35 people have seven or more Arches
It is also rare to have a full set of one of type of fingerprint:
10x Ulnar Loops (4%) – about 1 in 25 people
10x Whorls (3%) – about 1 in 34 people
10x Arches (women) (0.4%) – about 1 in 250 women
10x Arches (men) (0.1%) – about 1 in 1000 men

A full set of any of the four Minor Dermatoglyphic patterns is very unlikely to be seen and almost certainly impossible for Radial Loops and Tented Arches. For example, if we average the samples from the five surveys above, we see this distribution for Tented Arches:

Tented Arch on the Thumb – 0.0006%
Tented Arch on the Little finger – 0.19%
Tented Arch on Ring finger – 0.3%
Tented Arch on the Middle finger – 1.5%

Because some fingerprints are (almost) never seen on some of the fingers, it is impossible to discern their significance.

Suggestions for the interpretations of these, as contained in books like *God Given Glyphs* by Jennifer Hirsch or *Lifeprints* by Richard Unger are therefore purely speculative. His contention that the Tented Arch is one of the four main fingerprint patterns is rendered completely untenable when we know how *extremely* rare the Tented Arch is on four of the digits.[3]

1. Cherrill FR *The Fingerprint System at Scotland Yard* (HMSO 1954)
2. Lambourne G *Pattern Diagnosis and Standardisation in Dermatoglyphics* Identification News Jan 1983
3. R Unger *Lifeprints* (Crossing Press 2007) pp. 20–24

Appendix Two: Embryogenesis of the Fingerprints

Some debate has arisen as to whether the lines form in the hand before the skin ridges – or whether the skin ridges can be said to form before the lines. In discussing this subject, we are indebted to the research of the many scientists who have had the unenviable task of examining the hands of human foetuses at very early stages of gestation. At seven weeks, for instance, the embryo is only about 27mm long *in toto*.

One thing that embryologists have ascertained for certain is that *the lines are formed before the foetus is capable of any movement of the hand*:

> Schauble (1933) found that the thenar crease was already present in embryos of 27mm length, i.e. at about 7 weeks gestation. The proximal and distal transverse creases were observed in 40mm embryos (about 9 weeks gestation). These observations were confirmed by Wurth (1937) who found that the flexion creases develop during the second and third embryonal month. Onset of spontaneous hand movements has not been observed in embryos of less than 11.5 weeks gestation (Humphrey 1964), i.e. after the flexion creases are formed. Wurth (1937) concluded that the flexion creases developed independently of palmar and finger movement.
>
> Schaumann & Alter: 'Dermatoglyphics in Medical Disorders', 1976, p 103–4

Milton Alter adds: "Palmar creases develop during the second and third month and are not influenced by bone and muscle formation or by movement of the hand in utero" (Alter, Medicine v46/1, 1966, p 35).

Neurological Development and the Hand

Thus, the three main lines of the hand form between the seventh and ninth weeks of gestation *before* the foetal hand is capable of any movement. There is a very simple reason for this – the muscles of the hand have not yet formed! Hence the foetal hand is not actually capable of being "folded" in any way.

Humphrey's 1964 study set out to investigate the neurological development of the foetus; of relevance to us are the tests he performed for neural reflexes in the hand. Interestingly, he discovered that it is the fingers that respond earliest with flexion movements, rather than the thumb. Although finger "twitching" occurs a little prior to this, he reports that full finger closure does not occur until 13–14 weeks menstrual age (= 11–12 weeks foetal age) and the first "true grasp" does not occur until 15.5–18.5 weeks menstrual age (= 13.5–16.5 foetal age).

In contrast, the thumb "does not respond regularly until 15 weeks (menstrual age) and has no active part in grasping until 25 weeks" (Humphrey 1964, p 115). This contrasts strongly with the fact that the thenar crease forms first within the hand – a significant anomaly for those who adhere to the "lines are formed by the folding action of the hand" theory. For instance, Popich & Smith assert that "the thenar crease is the consequence of the oppositional function of the thumb and the thenar pad", despite the fact that they too found all the lines of the hand to be present by 11 weeks of gestation. Their criticisms of Humphrey's work overlooked this important finding.

Humphrey also outlines the development of the nerve endings in the hand and demonstrates that the nerve endings within the epidermis develop at the same time as the three main lines (9–11.5 weeks menstrual age, 7–9.5 weeks foetal age). This is important as a second reason why the lines cannot be formed by folding because in addition to the absence of muscles, *there is also the absence of nerve endings to stimulate any muscles*. The lines form before and at the same time as the hand is becoming muscularly and neurologically active. Humphrey's research gives further impetus for supporting a neurological thesis for the origins of the lines of the hand.

Dermatoglyphic Development

There are various hypotheses for the origin of the dermatoglyphic patterns within the hand of the foetus. The general view is based around the observation of the "volar pads" on the palm and on the end of the fingers. It is to be presumed that the "droplets" and the "mounts" that we see in the palm are the residue of these foetal "volar pads". These are quite large in the foetus – "comparable in relative size to a cherry on an adult fingertip" (Thompson & Thompson 1973, p 322). The theory is that it is the growth of these pads which causes the development of the dermatoglyphics into particular patterns, such as the whorl, the loop and the arch etc. When this occurs, seems open to debate. Whilst the foetal pads form early on, it is not clear at what stage during the deflation of these "lumps" that the fingerprint patterns actually appear:

> The hand of a 10 week human foetus bears conspicuous volar pads... At about the thirteenth week these pads begin to regress and during the period of regression the dermal ridges differentiate in the thickening skin. (Thompson & Thompson 1973)

> Ridges develop in relation to volar pads. The latter are evident at about the sixth week of gestation and reach maximal size by the 12th–13th week. *At this time* [my emphasis], patches of elevated ridges become evident and grow and coalesce as the volar pads regress. By the fourth month the epidermal ridges are well developed but the process is not complete before the sixth month. (Alter, 1966)

> The formation of the ridges takes place at an early stage in foetal life, beginning at the third month and continuing during the fourth.... When patterns occur, they are found on the site of the volar pads. These pads appear during the sixth and seventh foetal weeks and begin to subside during the fourth foetal month.... Ridges do not appear on the skin surface until about the 18th week. (Holt 1973, p 472)

> The epidermal patterns are formed early in foetal life. At about the 12th week of gestation undulations appear on the inner surface of the epidermis. It is these undulations which later develop into a structure of ridges and furrows that contain the ducts of sweat glands, whose pores are spaced along the surface of the ridges. (Penrose, 1969, p 73)

The consensus would seem to be that whilst the volar pads form around the 6th–7th weeks, the dermatoglyphics themselves do not *begin* to form until the 12th–13th weeks; they are not *finished* being formed until sometime after that, during the 16th–18th weeks. Holt seems quite certain that they do not appear on the skin's surface until that time. In other words, whilst the three main lines on the hand are all visible by the 11th week of gestation, the skin ridges are not apparent until some 5–7 weeks later.

Kimura and Kitagawa

In their research paper "Embryological Development of Human Palmar, Plantar and Digital Flexion Creases" (*Anatomical Recorder,* 1986), Kimura and Kitagawa's study showed that "the creases of the hand and foot of foetuses develop independently of flexion movements". Whilst they were aware of the two different hypotheses regarding the origins of the lines (that the lines are formed by flexion movements or not) their observations "support the second hypothesis which proposes that the creases develop independently of palmar and finger movement". In addition, they state:

> Most creases appear by 13 weeks of gestation... (whilst) the epidermal ridges are first laid down at approximately 13 weeks. Most creases, therefore, appear before the appearance of ridges.

Their extensive study of the hands of 160 human foetuses conclusively confirmed that the lines form *before* the skin ridges.

References

Alter M "Dermatoglyphic Analysis as a Diagnostic Tool" *Medicine* vol46/1 1966, pp. 35–55

Holt S "The Significance of Dermatoglyphics in Medicine" *Clinical Paediatrics* vol12/8 Aug 1973, pp. 471–484

Humphrey T "Some correlations between the appearance of human foetal reflexes and the development of the nervous system" *Prog Brain Res* 4 1963, p 93ff

Kimura S & Kitagawa T "Embryological development of human palmar, plantar and digital flexion creases" *Anatomical Recorder* 216, 1986, pp. 191–7

Penrose LS "Dermatoglyphics" *Scientific American* vol 221 1969, pp. 72–84

Popich G & Smith D "The genesis and significance of digital and palmar hand creases" *Journal of Paediatrics*, vol 77/6 Dec 1970

Schaumann & Alter "Dermatoglyphics in Medical Disorders" Ch 5 (Springer 1976)

Stevens C et al. "Development of human palmar and digital flexion creases" *Journal of Paediatrics*, July 1988, pp. 128–132

Thompson & Thompson "Genetics in medicine" *Dermatoglyphics in Medical Genetics* pp. 320–332 (Saunders 1973)

Bibliography

Chirological and Dermatoglyphic Books

Brandon-Jones, D Your Palm, Barometer of Health (Rider 1985)

Bridges BC, Practical Fingerprinting (Funk & Wagnalls 1942)

Cummins & Midlo, Fingerprints, Palms & Soles (Dover 1943)

Fincham J, The Spellbinding Power of Palmistry (Green Magic 2005)

Galton F, Fingerprints (Macmillan 1892)

Galton F, Fingerprint Directories (Macmillan 1895)

Gettings F, The Book of the Hand (Hamlyn 1965)

Holt SB, The Genetics of Dermal Ridges (Springfield 1968)

Hutchinson B, Your Life in Your Hands (Sphere 1967)

Jaquin N, The Hand of Man (Faber & Faber 1933)

Jaquin N, The Signature of Time (Faber & Faber 1940)

Jaquin N, The Hand Speaks (London 1942)

Loesch DZ, Quantitative Dermatoglyphics (OUP 1983)

Penrose LS, Recent Advances in Human Genetics (Churchill 1961)

Penrose LS, Biology of Mental Defect (Churchill 1963)

Penrose & Smith, Down's Anomaly (Churchill 1966)

Schaumann & Alter, Dermatoglyphics in Medical Disorders (Springer 1976)

Thompson, Genetics in Medicine (Saunders 1973)

Valentine GH, The Chromosomes & their Disorders (Heinemann 1986)

Selected References to Articles from Academic, Medical and Scientific Journals

Achs et al, Unusual dg findings associated with Rubella Embryopathy New Eng J Med v274 1966

Beckman et al, Fingers & palms in schizophrenia Acta Genet v13 1964

Cascos AS, Fingerprint patterns in Congenital Heart Disease Br Heart J v26 1964

Cascos AS, Palm print patterns in Congenital Heart Disease Br Heart J v27 1965

Dankmeijer J, Anthropological data on dermatoglyphics Am J Phys Anthr v23 1938

David TJ, Ridges off the End Syndrome Human Heredity v21 1971

David TJ, Ridge Dissociation & R.O.E.S Human Heredity v23 1973

Forbes A, Dermatoglyphics & palmar flexion creases in gonadal dysgenesis & Klinefelter's Syndrome New Eng J Med v270 1964

Furuhata et al, Man with no classifiable papillar ridge patterns Proc Jap Acad v26 1950

Gottlieb et al, Dermatoglyphic evidence for a congenital syndrome of early onset constipation Gastroenterology Aug 1986

Habibullah et al, Fingertip & palmar patterns in duodenal ulceration Human Heredity v32 1982

Hale et al, Features of Palmar Dermatoglyphics in Congenital Heart Disease J.A.M.A. v176 1961

Holt SB, Inheritance of Total Finger Ridge Count Ann Eugenics v17 1952

Holt SB, The significance of dermatoglyphics in medicine Clin Paediatr v12 1973

Lambourne G, Pattern Diagnosis and Standardisation in Dermatoglyphics Identification News Jan 1983

Mellor CS, Dermatoglyphics in schizophrenia Br J Psychiatry v114 1968

Menser, Dermatoglyphics in adults with congenital rubella Lancet 20 Jul 1968

Menser et al, Dermatoglyphic defects in children with leukaemia Lancet 31 May 1969

Newman HH, The fingerprints of twins J Genetics v23 1930

Newman HH, Palm print pattern in twins J Heredity v24 1931

Penrose LS, Creases on the minimal digit Lancet 12 Sep 1931

Penrose LS, Fingerprints, palms & chromosomes Nature v197 1963

Penrose LS, The distal triradius 't' in the hands of parents & siblings of mongol imbeciles Ann Hum Gen v19 1954

Purvis-Smith SG, Dermatoglyphic defects in children with leukaemia Lancet 31 May 1969

Purvis Smith SG, The Sydney Line Aust Paediatr J v8 1972

Raphael T & L, Fingerprints in schizophrenia J.A.M.A v180 1962

Sank D, Dermatoglyphics of childhood schizophrenia Acta Genet v18 1968

Seltzer et al, Fingerprint patterns in early and late onset primary degenerative dementia Arch. Neurology v43 1986

Slater E, Diagnosis of zygosity by fingerprints Acta Psych Scand v39 1963

Stiano et al, Prevalence of digital arches in children with abdominal pain & constipation J Pediatrics v117 1990

Takashina et al, Palmar Dermatoglyphics in Heart Disease J.A.M.A 29 Aug 1966

Weinreb HJ, Fingerprint patterns in Alzheimers Disease Arch. Neurology Jan 1985

Wolf et al Aplasia of dermal ridge patterns Lancet 26 Sep 1963

Wolff C The hand of the mental defective Br J Med Psych 1944

Wolff C The form & dermatoglyphs of the hands of 115 difficult and high grade boys Br J Med Psych 1947

A more extensive bibliography of articles on medical dermatoglyphics can be found in Schaumann & Alter's *Dermatoglyphics in Medical Disorders*.

O-BOOKS

SPIRITUALITY

O is a symbol of the world, of oneness and unity; this eye represents knowledge and insight. We publish titles on general spirituality and living a spiritual life. We aim to inform and help you on your own journey in this life.
If you have enjoyed this book, why not tell other readers by posting a review on your preferred book site?

Recent Bestsellers from O-Books Are:

Heart of Tantric Sex
Diana Richardson
Revealing Eastern secrets of deep love and intimacy to Western couples.
Paperback: 978-1-90381-637-0 ebook: 978-1-84694-637-0

Crystal Prescriptions
The A-Z guide to over 1,200 symptoms and their healing crystals
Judy Hall
The first in the popular series of eight books, this handy little guide is packed as tight as a pill bottle with crystal remedies for ailments.
Paperback: 978-1-90504-740-6 ebook: 978-1-84694-629-5

Shine On

David Ditchfield and J S Jones

What if the after effects of a near-death experience were undeniable? What if a person could suddenly produce high-quality paintings of the afterlife, or if they acquired the ability to compose classical symphonies? Meet: David Ditchfield.

Paperback: 978-1-78904-365-5 ebook: 978-1-78904-366-2

The Way of Reiki

The Inner Teachings of Mikao Usui

Frans Stiene

The roadmap for deepening your understanding of the system of Reiki and rediscovering your True Self.

Paperback: 978-1-78535-665-0 ebook: 978-1-78535-744-2

You Are Not Your Thoughts

Frances Trussell

The journey to a mindful way of being, for those who want to truly know the power of mindfulness.

Paperback: 978-1-78535-816-6 ebook: 978-1-78535-817-3

The Mysteries of the Twelfth Astrological House

Fallen Angels

Carmen Turner-Schott, MSW, LISW

Everyone wants to know more about the most misunderstood house in astrology — the twelfth astrological house.

Paperback: 978-1-78099-343-0 ebook: 978-1-78099-344-7

Feng Shui Your Way to Abundance
Janine Lowe
Feng Shui Your Way to Abundance shows how to use Feng Shui to attract positive energy and change into your life.
Paperback: 978-1-80341-674-8 ebook: 978-1-80341-683-0

Naked in the Now
Marijke McCandless
What if getting present was less like work and more like being seduced by a lover?
Paperback: 978-1-80341-567-3 ebook: 978-1-80341-574-1

Crystal Creed
Jamie Inglett
A beginner's guide to learning the sacred healing powers of crystals
Paperback: 978-1-80341-438-6 ebook: 978-1-80341-439-3

Revealing Light
Maryann Weston
YouTube psychic-astrologer Maryann Weston, from Revealing Light, shares her spiritual evolution after cancer had activated dormant psychic gifts, revealing a new purpose...
Paperback: 978-1-80341-730-1 ebook: 978-1-80341-738-7

Temple of Love
Natalie Glebova
The secret to true love is closer than you think.
Paperback: 978-1-80341-784-4 ebook: 978-1-80341-810-0